THE INTENTIONAL SALES MANAGER

THE INTENTIONAL SALES MANAGER

Harness the Power of *Purposeful Leadership* to Transform Your Team

Pat McManamon

Foreword by **David Mattson**

© 2019 Sandler Systems, Inc. All rights reserved.

Reproduction, modification, storage in a retrieval system or retransmission, in any form or by any means, electronic, mechanical, or otherwise, is strictly prohibited without the prior written permission of Sandler Systems, Inc.

S Sandler Training (with design), Sandler, and Sandler Selling System are registered service marks of Sandler Systems, Inc.

Paperback: 978-0-578-58153-8

E-book: 978-0-578-58154-5

I dedicate this book to my wife Michele, who has supported me throughout my career, notably through the entrepreneurial twitch that led me to Sandler and, ultimately, to the task of writing this book. Her support and partnership through this process has given me the strength to persevere and the confidence to stretch beyond my comfort zone.

CONTENTS

Acknowledgments   *ix*
Foreword   *xi*

1. Read This First   1
2. "That Needs to Change"   7
3. The Sand Trap   15
4. How to Alienate Salespeople   21
5. Meet Owen Mills   33
6. Whose Issue Is It?   45
7. One-on-One   53
8. Goal Time vs. Clock Time   63
9. The Attitude Shift   77
10. The Antidote to Paranoia   85
11. The Breakthrough   91
12. The Question of Questions   99
13. "I Want to Be You"   107
14. Turning the Corner   115
15. The Team Meeting, Transformed   131
16. The Self-Correcting Team   141

    Epilogue   155

ACKNOWLEDGMENTS

I owe a deep debt of gratitude to more people than I can name here, but the following list will have to do. My thanks go out first to David Mattson for leading Sandler Training into the position it holds today as the leading sales development organization in the world and also for his ongoing commitment to convert our collective experience into books from which the world can learn about Sandler's tremendous positive impact on people and organizations.

My gratitude is due also to Yusuf Toropov for his guidance, patience, and wisdom in bringing this manuscript across the finish line; to the staff at the Sandler home office for their daily assistance in running the business, and in particular to Rachel Miller, Margaret Stevens Jacks, Jennifer Willard, and Jasamine Stephens for their ongoing support of, and many contributions to, this project; to Jerry Dorris for the fantastic layout and design work; and to Lori Ames for her help in reviewing the manuscript and for a great promotion plan.

I would also like to thank my many friends in the Sandler network for the camaraderie, for the sharing of ideas and best practices, and for the continuous growth mind-set that has become a hallmark of the Sandler experience. In addition, I must send a word of heartfelt gratitude to my son John, my daughter Stephanie, and my son-in-law Austin for their great feedback during the many chapter "read-throughs"; to my clients, who collectively provided the experiences and examples that allowed me to develop the characters in this book; to my office colleagues, who kept me on task, freed up my time, and offered the advice, guidance, and support I needed to complete this project; to the many true friends who supported me along the way, even when it wasn't easy to do so; and to my dear friend Howard, for the encouragement to push ahead when the process seemed to stall.

FOREWORD

The transition from salesperson to sales leader can be a deeply challenging one, not least because the job description for the sales leader is so frequently misunderstood. The deliverables of the two positions are entirely different, but many in sales often treat them as though they were very closely related. As a result, people who are promoted from the position of sales contributor to the position of team leader often find themselves struggling. This is not surprising. They are navigating unfamiliar territory, often falling back on behaviors that don't seem to connect to the complex, demanding job of understanding, motivating, and leading a sales team.

It's one of the sad truths of business life that most people tasked with the responsibility of managing a sales team receive little or no formal guidance when it comes to addressing the essential question: "How do I succeed in this job?" Pat McManamon's book fills this gap. It offers some clear, powerful, and compelling answers to this question, and it shares the big ideas that help managers to make the transition to the kind of purposeful, intentional leadership that leads to personal fulfillment—and financial success—on both the individual and team levels. It's essential reading for everyone tasked with leading a sales team.

David Mattson
President/CEO, Sandler Training

CHAPTER 1

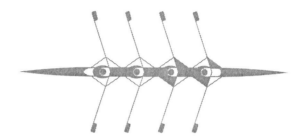

Read This First

"Sales manager."

These two words encompass what is arguably the most challenging role within any company. In my experience, it is also the most misunderstood role.

What follows is a story about a sales manager who experienced and, by harnessing the power of intention, overcame some of the most common challenges faced by the managers I have worked with over the years. The causes of these challenges are many, but most of them, I have found, start with a fundamental confusion about the very role of a manager.

A manager is not a salesperson. These are two totally different roles. Sometimes it's easy to lose sight of that. The manager's job is not to close sales. Very often, however, they act with the intention of closing sales. This common problem is compounded by the reality that the metrics that can create a viable scorecard for salespeople are a little harder to identify at the management level.

Managers who become truly effective as leaders of sales teams embrace their management role by establishing for themselves minimum standards of performance and activity that are very different from what salespeople are expected to do. These standards connect to the goals of developing their people and coaching them so that they get better at executing what they know how to do. This embrace of the sales manager's role does not happen without a consistent, disciplined effort guided by intentional decisions.

intentional
/inˈten(t)SH(ə)n(ə)l/
adjective
done on purpose; deliberate.

This book, then, is all about intentional sales management—management done on purpose, with decisions made consciously, rather than from sheer force of habit. Note: The intention of a successful manager is not the same as the intention of a successful salesperson.

My hope is that this book will help current and aspiring sales managers see the potential hazards of not being focused and intentional when it comes to developing their people and themselves. My aim is to support them as they inspire others to leverage their personal goals as a means of sustaining their own continuous growth by encouraging the continuous growth of others.

While writing this book, I found myself reflecting on the countless sales teams I've worked with over the years. I realized that there was an all-too-common theme among teams that found themselves in trouble and looked to us for help: managers and salespeople who held themselves and their organizations back because they could not see their own blind spots, and were not ready to set up a plan—an intention—for overcoming them.

Being intentional as a sales manager means accepting that you and others are going to have overlooked areas where there is room for improvement and then working from there without judgment or drama. This is not only part of being a successful leader but also part of being a successful human being. There is always something to learn, something to improve, something to see more clearly. Of course, it's possible, and perhaps even likely, that you as a manager may notice the blind spots of others before you recognize your own. I'm hoping this book will help you to address that challenge as well. If, as you read, you find yourself recognizing familiar problem areas in people you work with and around (and, of course, you will), here is my advice: Don't dwell on their shortcomings. Don't compare what they're doing to what you might do in a similar situation. Don't pat yourself on the back. Remember, that's not your role. Instead, ask, "If I were to be intentional about helping this person to get better, what is the one thing I could do that would help them most?" And then take action.

Big Ideas

- This book is all about intentional sales management—management done on purpose, with decisions made consciously, not from sheer force of habit.
- Being intentional as a sales manager means accepting that you and others are going to have overlooked areas where there is room for improvement and then working from there without judgment or drama.

Be Intentional about Reading This Book

Whenever you encounter an idea or insight in these pages that might be able to help you, make a written note of it. Keep a journal, a notebook, a digital file, or some other form of written record of the ideas and insights you want to implement. You will find a summary section at the end of each chapter. You might want to start by writing down one of the insights from the "Big Ideas" box you just read.

CHAPTER 2

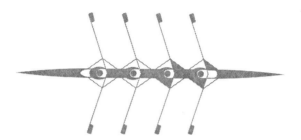

"That Needs to Change"

Tom, sales manager for Bradgate, scrawled doodles of golf courses and fairways on his yellow legal pad. As the meeting droned on, he was finding it harder and harder to stay engaged—even though it was his own meeting.

One of his salespeople, Stace, was delivering a lengthy monologue about why a big deal had been delayed, why she still felt good about it, and how the project would definitely be moving forward sometime soon. Tom had lost interest in this topic some time ago, and was thinking now about what it would be like to play against the greatest golfers in the world.

What, he wondered, was Augusta National really like? Are the greens even smoother than they look on TV?

There was a lengthy silence, and Tom realized that Stace had completed her weekly update. Everyone in the room was now looking at him.

"Right," Tom said. "Thanks for that, Stace. I believe that's the last of the updates for today, yes?"

Everyone seated around the conference table nodded.

"OK—great meeting, everybody. Keep your eye on the ball this week. Now, let's go get 'em!"

Tom clapped his hands briskly to adjourn the meeting. As was customary, the members of the team smiled, clapped once in their customary imitation of Tom, and headed out the door in slow procession.

Later that afternoon, Tom took part in a big meeting with J.D., the owner of Bradgate; Mike, the CFO; and Debbie, the operations manager. J.D. called these meetings quarterly to ensure that his team was on plan for all their stated goals. This was a higher-risk discussion than his sales meeting earlier, Tom knew, and he would have to push any fleeting thoughts of golf and glory to the side. He would need to focus. He turned to a new sheet on his legal pad. He did not doodle.

Mike's presentation was crisp and right to the point. In line with J.D.'s stated goal of containing costs, improving margins, increasing operations efficiencies, and increasing revenues,

Mike announced that Bradgate's costs were down 5% for the previous year despite an increase in headcount. He flashed a broad grin as he said this. Tom took notes.

Debbie, the operations manager, reported that the effects of the Six Sigma training had taken hold and that productivity was up 12%, exceeding the operating efficiency metric. She noted with some concern that inventory was starting to build. If orders didn't increase according to plan, all the gains of the past six months could be wiped out by warehouse expenses. She cast a meaningful glance at Tom, who had been taking notes on all this, too.

"You're up, Tom," said J.D., in a tone that seemed oddly flat and unemotional to Tom.

Tom smiled, stood, and made his way to the front of the room. He fired up his PowerPoint presentation. It was a real beauty. There were plenty of colorful charts, graphs, and detailed analyses of individual salespeople's performance.

Tom started summarizing his blizzard of color-coded bullet points with all the drive and passion and polish he generally displayed on such occasions. But, just a few minutes into his presentation, J.D. put up his hand and said, "Alright, Tom—enough with the dog and pony show. Are you on plan with your revenue goals, and if not, why not?"

A tense silence hung over the room. Tom looked in J.D.'s direction to size up just how bad this was likely to be, and the initial signals were not good. His boss's gaze was fixed and unyielding, and his arms were crossed. This was not going to be pretty.

There was going to be no tap-dancing around it. Tom was in trouble. He was not on plan, not even close to it—and, even worse, he had no idea why.

For the past three months, he had been pushing his salespeople to perform, imploring them to sell more, to bring in new deals, and generally to pick up the pace. They all said they understood what he was saying and they all promised to do everything they could, but the results, and even worse, the sense of the urgency, were nonexistent. Tom simply didn't know what to do to motivate them.

"We're way off target," Tom finally said. "At least 15 percent. Maybe 20."

Tom's stomach churned. He could hear it, and he was pretty sure everyone else could, too.

J.D. cleared his throat louder than absolutely necessary and, after a glacial pause, said, "Tom, what seems to be the problem? You assured us that the sales goal was attainable, and that you were up to the task. What's going on?"

What *was* going on? Tom began to reflect on the sales activities in the first half of the year and asked himself what was different from the previous year. The answer that came back was that the team was at fault. Simple as that. They had lost a step.

They had become complacent. They hadn't listened to him when he said in no uncertain terms that they needed to step up their game.

The current year's numbers, he knew, were soft. They were harbingers of a mediocre performance throughout the entire fiscal year to come if Tom didn't make some changes—and fast. But what kinds of changes could he make with a team that simply wouldn't take action?

Tom realized that his counterparts in operations and finance—now staring at him with blank expressions—had taken drastic measures and implemented major changes in their departments to deliver according to their plan objectives. His sales team and their activities, by contrast, had not changed tactics one bit.

J.D. was still looking at him in pained silence. Mike and Debbie were as well. Time to get real.

"Well," Tom said, "it's common knowledge that Chatfield, our number one competitor, has taken a very aggressive position in building market share. I guess you know our deliveries have been behind schedule because of the overstock problems in the warehouse. Operations needs to tighten things up. We probably need to review our pricing on high-volume items, too. My gut tells me we are losing orders due to pricing."

"Is that it?" J.D. interrupted in an irritated tone.

"Yes, for now," Tom replied. But then (against his own better judgment), he added, "I do feel like the economy will be better in the second half, J.D. We will be able to make up for these soft results we are seeing in the first half of the year."

J.D. sat quietly studying his notepad for 20 seconds, which felt like an eternity to Tom. Finally, he said, "Mike, Debbie. You guys can go now. Tom, stick around, will you?"

Mike and Debbie couldn't gather up their things and leave fast enough. Tom watched as they scrambled out the door and wished that he could escape with them.

When they were gone, J.D. looked Tom in the eye and said, "I'm struggling with what just happened. I feel like you've put me and the whole company in a bad position. We hired staff and increased inventory based on the plan we all committed to at last year's planning meeting. It's clear to me that you're not taking this problem seriously. To add to the problem, you just attempted to make the kinds of lame excuses I'd expect to hear from a struggling salesperson, not a senior leader."

J.D. stood up and pulled his suit jacket from the hanger on the back of the door. As he reached for the handle, he turned to Tom and said, "By Wednesday of next week, I want a detailed report from you on each team member's new goal and a comprehensive plan that shows me exactly how you're going to turn the situation around. I wouldn't have hired you for this job if I didn't think you were capable, Tom. But right now, it's clear to me you are not focused. You're not leading the team—the team is leading you. That dynamic needs to change. And I need you to commit to changing it."

And with that, he opened the door and walked out.

> **Big Ideas**
>
> - Effective leaders don't make excuses.
> - If you are not leading the team, the team is leading you.
> - If the dynamic needs to change, you as the leader must commit to changing it.

Be Intentional about Professional Development

Here's a question to consider. Most managers acknowledge the importance of professional development for the members of their team, but how many managers are actually intentional about developing themselves professionally? In my experience, it's only a small percentage.

Here's what happens. As managers move higher in their organization, they feel more pressure to produce results—and often resort to working longer hours in the hope of achieving more. If working more doesn't work, they resort to working harder. While this is playing out, they have little to no time to even consider professional development. Ultimately they recognize this deficiency and vow to address the problem "when I find the time." That time is never found.

This common cycle sends the wrong message to their people. It implies that managers are above the growth and development stage, which most people would acknowledge is the farthest thing from the truth. Committing to your own personal professional development plan and being intentional about carrying it out is vital to the culture of your team and essential to supporting its capacity to grow.

CHAPTER 3

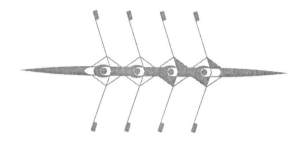

The Sand Trap

Despite Tom's best efforts over the weekend to forget about all that had been going wrong recently, the subject of work came up during the third hole of his regular Saturday morning golf match.

Santiago, the best golfer in the group, asked, "How's business, Tom?"

Tom's first instinct was to say "Great!" and bluster on from there about long-term trends and pending initiatives, which was what he usually did when someone asked him this question. But something inside told him that really wasn't what he needed to do right now. He looked Santiago in the eye and saw genuine concern.

He knew that Santiago shared many of the same contacts he did, and he wondered whether his golfing buddy might already have heard that things were not going well. Even if that hadn't been the case, though, something about Santiago's expression told him that blustering his way through his problems wasn't the way to go this morning.

As he put his tee in the ground, Tom said, "Things could be better. Our sales are flat, margins are shrinking, and my salespeople don't seem to be trying all that hard. Frankly, they've let me down. And I'm sick of it." There. He'd said it.

But something in Tom's demeanor, or perhaps his tone of voice, must have told Santiago that he had hit a nerve. Santiago quickly changed the subject to how well the course was coming back after its recent treatment.

That morning, Tom's golf game served only as an intermittent distraction from a steady stream of ominous thoughts about work.

Did the sales team know the severity of the situation? Some of them were in real danger of losing their jobs. For that matter, Tom could conceivably lose his own job or almost as troubling, be held personally responsible for the whole company missing the bonus that was tied to the plan the members of the executive team had all agreed to for this calendar year.

The Sand Trap

Why am I the one feeling all the heat? Tom stewed as he tried to fish another one of his shots out of the water. *It's the salespeople who need to step up and deliver. Clearly they are the problem.* He swung, more than a little distracted. The ball landed in a sand trap.

I've had it with the excuses, the complaints, and the objections, he thought. *I'm meeting with them on Monday morning and I'm putting the heat on them for a change. I'm tired of covering for them. I'm demanding that they each show me a workable plan for making quota—and then I'm going to insist that they each start working the plan. Things are going to change, and that's that!*

He stalked toward the ball, full of resolve. If only he could extract a shot from a sand trap with half the skill Santiago brought to that problem, he might be able to salvage a bogey.

> **Big Ideas**
> - Blaming the team is not effective leadership.
> - Playing the victim is not effective leadership.
> - Demanding that the members of your team create a plan before you have created a plan is not effective leadership.

Be Intentional about Who's Really Responsible

As a manager, it must be your priority to develop your people and your priority to accept personal responsibility for the results your team delivers. A strong manager accepts the outcomes of all activities in their department as the result of something the manager either did or didn't do.

This responsible approach to managing opens you up to learning from failures, and sets your intention on a path of continuous improvement. Once this mindset is the norm, once it is modeled consistently by you (the manager), the staff can come to recognize and respect responsibility as the default mindset—and it becomes part of the culture. But you, the manager, must display this mindset first.

It may be tempting to blame the members of the sales team for results that don't match what you expected. But doing so is counterproductive because it keeps you from embracing learning opportunities, being transparent with your team about what you've learned, and showing that you accept the responsibility for the team's performance. When this kind of thinking starts

> from the manager's side, and not before, the department is positioned to achieve significant growth.

CHAPTER 4

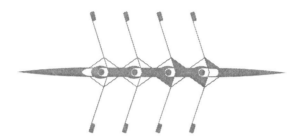

How to Alienate Salespeople

On Monday morning, Tom gathered the sales team together in the conference room.

"I'm going to need your full attention, please," he said, in what he hoped was a brisk and commanding tone of voice. "That means no texting and no emails. Clear?"

Tom cleared his throat for emphasis and waited for the room to settle down. After about 30 seconds, everyone who had gathered around the table got the message and all the phones were discreetly put away.

"Thanks," Tom said. "Now here's the scoop. I just got my

head handed to me at the senior leadership meeting. All the other departments are meeting or exceeding the plan objectives. Our numbers, on the other hand, are lagging way behind of last year in terms of both top line revenue and margin. So my question for you is: How do you feel about that?"

The room fell silent. Suddenly all assembled seemed very interested in the condition of their shoe tops, the cleanliness of their fingernails, or the view of the parking lot provided by the conference room window.

"This was supposed to be our year for growth," Tom said, a little too loudly. "I really don't understand what happened here, but I do know we all need to pull our socks up, starting immediately. So listen up. We're going to look at each person's numbers now, with a microscope."

As her manager Tom droned on about her numbers and her sales pipeline and the importance of stepping up, Keiko drifted in and out of what he was saying. She was the company's top producer, and she knew it.

When she bothered to pretend to pay attention to Tom's little lecture, she nodded attentively, and she was experienced enough with this kind of meeting to do so at the right moments. When she didn't, she surveyed the people sitting at the table to identify her own list of nominees for the worst offenders for the underperformance of the past quarter .

Surely, Keiko thought, *Tom doesn't need to worry about me.*

She consistently led the team in revenue for the past two years, and she regularly made her revenue goals. But Tom was looking at her with a meaningful arch of his eyebrows as he went on rambling about her targets and her commitment.

Keiko looked away.

She had started with Bradgate four years ago. Having come from the industry, she personally knew many of the decision makers at large accounts and had been able to convert a couple that she had sold at her prior company. Keiko prided herself on developing a strong bond with her customers. On more than one occasion, Tom had requested that she spend more time looking for new clients and allow the inside sales and customer support team to take the lead role in answering customer questions and resolving problems. Tom had even pressed the issue. Just last week, he had taken her out to lunch for the sole reason of pointing out that 85% of her quota was being met by just three accounts. Tom kept harping on the fact that her total book of business consisted of over 115 companies, many of which had the potential of being just as large as the top three producing accounts.

Despite the evidence presented by her sales manager, though, Keiko countered with comments like this: "If I neglect my main customers while trying to grow new accounts, I'm going to lose them to the competition. As long as I hit my goal, it shouldn't matter how I get it."

The implication, as always, was that the department's numbers would be even worse if she followed Tom's advice—which she never did.

Besides, Keiko thought now, as she stared past Tom and his seemingly endless lecture, *why would he want to mess with me of all people? And in public? Why shouldn't he use a meeting like this to put the heat on the salespeople who aren't hitting their numbers, like Ryan?*

It was true enough that Ryan wasn't hitting his numbers lately, but even as Tom rambled on about his various numbing metrics and all the pressure he was feeling from J.D. and the folks in Finance and Operations about people like Ryan stepping up, Ryan had already convinced himself that this latest emergency had absolutely nothing to do with him.

I've been with Bradgate the longest of anybody at this table, he thought, *including Tom. It's true I've been in a slump lately, but I've had some good quarters, too, where I crushed my numbers. It would be nice if sometimes management would recognize my value beyond sales production.*

Tom shot him a glance, as though to make sure he was paying close enough attention to this long, boring, condescending speech. Ryan sat up a little straighter and pretended to listen in.

I hope the sales support group and operations people remember, Ryan thought, his face a mask of attentive compliance, *that whenever they're struggling with understanding a customer's* request, how often they count on me to sort things out. Most of the time, it's not even a customer in my territory. And once, just once, I'd like to get a 'thank you' from one of the salespeople whose account I helped to save."

Ryan locked onto Tom's monologue just long enough to hear him say, "Ryan, you must have noticed that Jason brought in a new major account last month, and that's the kind of thing we're going to need to see a lot more of from you, too, if you're going to make a statement this quarter."

Ryan winced. *Sure,* he thought, *make Jason the hero. There's another example of me saving the day and not getting any credit.* Last week he had spent 45 minutes helping one of Jason's accounts—while Jason was out meeting with big prospects and hogging all the glory.

Jason had been Tom's outside salesperson for just over a year, having come from the inside sales department. He had a reputation as a hard worker—someone who was always fully dedicated to the task at hand, whatever it might be. As Tom delivered his speech about the importance of everyone on the team hunkering down and hitting the numbers, Jason was engaged and taking plenty of notes. As he wrote, a familiar, eternally optimistic smile beamed from his young face.

Tom winced when he saw it. He recognized that clueless smile. He had told Jason many times that he was spending too much time chasing bad prospects and creating proposals for unqualified opportunities. Every time he'd made these points, he'd seen that smile and heard Jason agree to change his approach. But nothing ever changed.

At least Jason was trying. At least he was showing up a little early and leaving a little bit after five thirty. Maybe, after today, Tom would encourage the others to get off their behinds and set some meetings.

Tom watched Jason scribble earnestly. The guy meant well, but his approach to the job was unsustainable. In the long run, he would burn out or just get discouraged and try another line of work. His closing rate was abysmal—the low teens.

"We need to work on improving our closing rate," Tom said, forcefully. Jason looked up and nodded with vigor, flashing that big smile of his.

Camila had heard all this before. Prior to joining Bradgate, she had experienced "manager's panic" firsthand—and paid the price.

When the market got soft in the mortgage business and then again in the IT staffing business, her sales managers had looked for opportunities to cull the herd. Camila knew the drill. About every two years, management would find some excuse to blame their department's lack of results on a few salespeople, even if the real problem had been a collapse in the economy, or the leaders of the company not having invested enough in lead generation, or a combination of the two. Whenever that happened (and so far it had happened to Camila three times), senior management had cut headcount so they could save their own bonuses. She had seen it play out herself.

Here we go again, she thought as she listened to Tom tear into her performance. *The buddy system will protect the salespeople who are making the numbers simply because they have better territories and better internal connections. People like me, people like Stace, who've only been around for a little while, will get all the pressure. Why? Because we haven't made our quota yet, even though that's not really our fault. What's the use? This happens to me every two years. I get fired for no reason. But at least I can see it coming now. My job now is to buy as much time as I can—and update my resume.*

She looked over her shoulder, toward the back of the room. *Poor Stace*, she thought. *She'll never know what hit her.*

Tom's eye fell on Stace, seated all the way at back of the room, who was avoiding eye contact with anyone.

This was Stace's first job out of college. A new hire, she had shown nothing but promise from the first phone call onward. Her resume had boasted a great GPA and lots of interesting work experience, And, she had sailed through the interview process. She had been (or so Tom thought at the time) an easy, excellent hire.

Stace was articulate and presented herself well—until, that is, she needed to speak with senior management or anyone she perceived to be of a higher level of authority. Then, she froze and became submissive, as though she were suddenly eager to follow any and all instructions.

The problem was, Stace simply couldn't think on her feet. She was masterful as long as you gave her plenty of time to prepare, and as long as you didn't ask her to challenge the preconceptions of anyone she considered to be an important person. But that wasn't how sales worked. If you wanted to succeed, you had to be able to improvise, and you had to find a way to present new perspectives and new possibilities in a compelling way, even to company leaders with fancy titles.

Once, in the break room, Tom had overheard Stace telling Camila about her strategy for securing great grades in college: "Make friends with every professor, and drop any course where it seems even remotely possible that you won't get an A."

That about summed it up. Stace was eager to please, and she was no risk taker. She had triumphed during the interview process not because she had the requisite skills and the temperament to succeed as a salesperson, but because interviews were something she could prepare for ahead of time and because she had gotten Tom to like her as a person. Or at least she thought she had.

Stace heard her name, and her blood ran cold. Her closing rate, it turned out, was nine percent. Less than one out of ten of her presentations turned into revenue. Tom pointed this out to the entire group.

Stace began wondering whether maybe Tom didn't like her after all.

A long pause had settled over conference room. Tom stared at the faces of his sales team. They all stared back at him, waiting for him to either keep talking or adjourn the meeting—with a clear preference for the latter.

Silently, Tom asked himself: *Do I really have the right team to achieve the goals I committed to?*

With a little more than six months left in the year, it would be very difficult to find replacements who could ramp up quickly enough to have any kind of impact. And what would J.D. think if Tom told him he had to make a lot of personnel changes?

With the sole exception of Ryan, Tom had hired all these people. Not only that, he had confirmed at the senior management retreat that his team was more than capable of hitting its sales goals.

Was it? Would he have to eat those words?

"OK," Tom said to his team. "That's it for now. Let's get out there and make something happen."

Everyone stood up and shuffled out of the room, leaving Tom and his chair at the head of the table. All he could do was stare up at the numbers he had written on the whiteboard and wonder if he was the right guy for the job.

> **Big Ideas**
>
> - Shining a public spotlight on (perceived) performance gaps during team meetings only causes resentment and disengagement.
> - Use group meetings to celebrate milestones met and achievements reached, and to tie those victories to forward progress on the group goal.

Be Intentional about Group Meetings

A critical mistake is demonstrated in this chapter: Attempting to address individual performance gaps in a group meeting.

Some managers claim that they do this because they want to use time efficiently; others may admit that they are uncomfortable with confronting the members of their staff about underperformance during one-on-one meetings. Whatever the justification, this strategy is simply not effective. It demotivates individuals and hurts team morale.

Managers must use one-on-one meetings to assess individual performance gaps, support salespeople as they take ownership of those gaps, help them connect the benefit of closing those gaps to the discomfort of change, and then help them identify what specific changes will take place and when. Once this is complete, the process of change is just beginning. Managers must consistently check with the individual about their progress and provide resources when necessary to help the employee on their personal growth journey.

CHAPTER 5

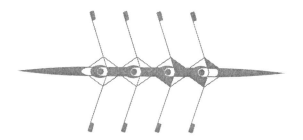

Meet Owen Mills

Wednesday morning, about an hour before lunch. Tom got up from his desk and went out to pour his third cup of coffee of the day. He didn't actually drink more than one cup a day, but he found checking the cubicles en route to the coffee pot to be a subtle, effective way to check in on his sales team.

He scanned the hall. Good. Only two of the five were in the office. The rest were out on sales calls—he hoped.

As he approached Jason's cubicle, Tom heard him on the phone trying to get a gatekeeper to grant him an appointment with the boss.

"Listen," Jason said. "I'm going to be in the area Tuesday and Wednesday of next week. Which would be better?"

What an overused technique, Tom thought to himself. *We've talked about it multiple times. Why is he still doing that? Well, at least he's putting in the effort. At least I can always depend on Jason to work hard.*

As Tom turned the corner, he saw Ryan in a conversation with Bradgate's operations manager. They were trying to resolve what looked like a recurring problem. The tone of the exchange was cordial but strained. Finally. An opportunity to demonstrate Tom's new-found intensity about making sure his team members hit their sales goal—and a chance to show the operations department he really was being tough on his people.

Tom stopped and said, "Ryan, what are you working on?"

Ryan looked up and began to explain. "A couple of my customers are complaining about the order entry system, and there's been a change in procedure that has been causing a delay in…"

Tom interrupted and said, "You don't have any orders, so why do you care?"

Ryan, who up to that point had been oblivious to the harsher intent behind Tom's entry into the conversation, froze for a moment. Then he shrugged, turned to the operations manager, and said, "I guess you're on your own." But as Ryan began to walk away, he muttered, loud enough to be heard, "It's kind of tough to sell new customers when you know their orders are going to be screwed up."

On Tom's way back from refilling his coffee cup, he stopped by Jason's desk and asked, "How's it going?"

Jason replied with his usual response: "Just grinding away." And smiled. When Tom didn't walk away and thus made it clear he was waiting for a more detailed response, Jason said, "I'm trying to get through this new prospect list and book some appointments."

Tom said, "That's great. Hey, I heard you as I was walking by talking to what sounded like an administrative assistant. Did you get that appointment?"

"We'll see," Jason said. "She has to check with the boss to see if he has time. I gave her two different days. I can't imagine there wouldn't be 30 minutes to meet with me. She asked me to send some literature, so that's a good sign. If her boss is interested she said she would let me know, and soon."

Tom sighed. "Don't you see what happened?" he asked. "We've talked about this, Jason. That's the oldest blow-off in the book. She is not going to call back and she probably won't even show literature to her boss. I'm surprised you're still falling for that."

And with that, Tom turned and walked back to his office, leaving Jason feeling dejected and confused. His next call didn't go any better.

Lunchtime already? Tom sent the message he had been working on and looked at his phone to verify that it really was noon. Where did the morning go? *I can't believe it took me all morning to reply to those Operations emails,* he thought. *What a waste of time. Meanwhile, I haven't heard from any of my people. The phones have been quiet all morning. This lack of communication is making me very uncomfortable. I need to get my mind off things. Maybe some food from the diner will help.*

Tom grabbed the morning paper, made sure the sports page was inside, and walked out to the parking lot. He gunned the engine and eased his Gran Torino onto the main road. In less than five minutes, he was in the parking lot of the Crossroads Diner. The place was busy.

"Well, look who's here," said Sam, the owner of the Crossroads, looking up from her grill, which was full and sizzling. "Haven't seen you in over a week," she said as Tom took his usual seat at the counter.

"Yeah," Tom replied, "I've been tied up in meetings and feeling a lot of pressure at work. Great to see you again, Sam. Sorry I've been missing in action. Tough week."

Sam smiled and said, "You'll get past it. You always do."

Tom shrugged and ordered his usual—a hot pastrami on rye and a Coke—and Sam jotted the order down. Then she was back to work, calling out orders to the wait staff and greeting customers. Tom opened the paper and settled into the sports section. Two minutes later, his sandwich and drink arrived, along with an extra dill pickle. Tom smiled. Clearly, Sam could tell that he really *was* having a hard time. The extra pickle was to let Tom know that Sam knew how to treat a regular customer.

About halfway through his meal, Tom noticed a fellow in a nice business suit poised to sit down next to him. As he collected his newspaper to make room, Tom heard the man say, "Are you Tom? J.D. said I might find you here. I'm Owen Mills. May I sit?"

Confused and a little curious, Tom said, "Sure, I guess. Have a seat."

Owen settled in, placed his order, and said, "I thought this would be a good place to get to know each other, as we may be spending some time talking shop. J.D. and I spoke a few days ago, and he filled me in on the company plan and the sales shortfall. If you're OK with it, I'd like to hear your take on the situation."

Tom took a deep breath. He knew J.D. often hired executive coaches and consultants, but it would've been nice to have gotten a little advanced warning. "Well, we're actually doing pretty well. We just need a couple of big wins and I figure we'll be back on track. Just out of curiosity, Owen, what exactly did J.D. share with you about my department?"

"I'll be happy to share that. Does it make sense for me to tell you what I do, and you can decide if we have anything further to talk about?"

Tom said, "Sure."

"Oftentimes, sales leaders share with me their frustrations about the lack of consistency and reliability of production from the sales group. It may be a concern about the pattern of winning business by discounting. Some of them are actually worried that frequent discounting with low closing ratios are fueling the competition."

So, J.D. knew what Tom was up against. That was a good sign, Tom guessed.

Owen went on: "I'm able to help those companies that are open enough to admit and recognize these problems. I do that by working with them to establish systems and processes that are repeatable and trackable. In short, I help them build an intentional sales culture, rather than a series of activities that are left to chance. Tom, does any of this make sense?"

"Sure, it does. You just described my sales department. I guess J.D. must have debriefed you pretty well. I didn't realize he knew that level of detail about what I was dealing with."

"That's funny," Owen said. "J.D. and I didn't even speak. He sent me a one-line text message and asked if I could determine if I thought you were the type of manager I could help. Years ago, I helped a neighbor of J.D.'s in a similar situation. That was before I started working directly with J.D."

"Interesting," Tom said. "What do you mean, the type

of manager you could help? Does your process not work for all companies?"

Owen smiled. "It's not the process that's the issue," he said. "It's the people, and specifically the leaders. If the management team isn't willing to recognize and admit their own role in creating gaps in performance or production or even to acknowledge that there is a problem, I can't help them. Their excuses about what's going on in the market, how tough the competition is, how the economy is preventing growth, how they never have enough resources—all of that is them externalizing the issue, and the sales team quickly picks up on that. And unfortunately, that becomes the acceptable norm in the working culture: making excuses."

"Does that happen a lot?" Tom asked, feeling a little uneasy. He knew Owen was basically describing Tom's own justifications during the last management meeting. It was a little like Owen had been eavesdropping somehow.

"You'd be surprised," Owen said. "Many managers, especially middle managers, are insecure in their role. They try to hide that insecurity by pretending to have it all figured out. They may stop learning or even stop admitting that they have any personal shortcomings, all for fear of appearing vulnerable."

"You don't say," Tom said.

"It happens a lot," Owen went on. "That's a shame, because it's a very dangerous mindset, and it often leads to major career problems."

"OK," Tom said. "I get it. What's next? How do you think you can help me?"

Owen looked a little surprised at this remark. "I'm not sure I can just yet, Tom. How do you see me helping?"

"Well, first of all, I know we need to have better systems for prospecting, selling, and account retention. We really are terribly inconsistent. I realize that. Secondly, we need to stop the random proposals and quotes to prospects who are not serious about leaving the incumbent relationship—or even qualified. Overall, we need to get committed to a sales plan instead of aimlessly, occasionally, chasing leads." Tom was more than a little impressed with his own summary of his team's problems. He sat back and waited for a response from Owen, but it took a surprisingly long time to show up. He seemed to be considering every syllable Tom had shared.

"OK," Owen said, finally. "I have to ask, though, do you really think this is important enough to fix?"

"Absolutely!" replied Tom, somewhat taken aback. Was there any doubt?

"I have to ask that because, frankly, it won't be easy to change habits. It won't be easy to hold yourself and others accountable. It won't be easy to reverse the pattern of excuse making. And it won't happen overnight. It will take some time and some effort to create a different culture. So with all that being said, are you committed? Think about this, please, before you answer one way or another."

"Yes," Tom said. "I'm all in."

Owen smiled. "Great," he said. "When we get back, I'll sort out the details with J.D."

When they had finished lunch, they agreed to head back to the office to get started. On their way out, Sam called out, "Go get 'em, Tom!"

"You know it, Sam," Tom said. And he followed Owen out the door.

> **Big Ideas**
>
> - Changing habits is difficult. Most people need the support of a coach to pull it off.
> - If the management team isn't willing to recognize and admit their own role in creating gaps in performance or production or even to acknowledge that there is a problem, coaching won't help.
> - When leadership externalizes and makes excuses, the sales team quickly picks up on that. That behavior then becomes the acceptable norm in the working culture: making excuses.

Be Intentional about Consistent, Ongoing Development

Intentional sales managers understand that their role in developing their people and helping them achieve their full potential is not something they can simply check off a to-do list and consider finished. It is an ongoing process. Each employee is different; each person who reports to the manager comes from a unique background with certain beliefs and habitual actions in place. Those beliefs and habitual actions, also referred to as "recordings" or "scripts," are hardwired in the human brain. Everyone has them. Once the manager identifies a script that is holding an employee back, the ideal intention is to help the person start noticing how the script works, when it comes into play, and what happens when it is followed heedlessly.

Being intentional about this process is an extended journey, not a brief walk in the park. It takes patience and tact on the manager's part to consistently point out when a recording is working against an employee, and it takes commitment and self-awareness on the employee's part to accept the manager's input.

Many of these scripts have been with people since

childhood. Changing them requires a deep personal resolve, one that must be supported by a powerful desire for a different outcome than what they've delivered in the past. They may need to give themselves conscious permission to think and do things differently. For both salespeople and managers, that may take a while. So think in terms of a cross-country journey, not a quick trip to the convenience store.

CHAPTER 6

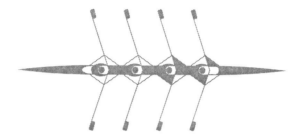

Whose Issue Is It?

Back at Tom's office, Owen closed the door and asked Tom to pull up the sales plan.

"You mean our sales goals?" Tom replied. "I've got that broken down by month." There was a note of pride in his voice. He had been focused on these monthly numbers with great intensity since that disastrous conference room meeting with J.D. He was pretty sure he could recite the monthly team and individual goals from memory.

"Yes," Owen said. "We'll need that as well. But I'm looking for the plan."

"What do you mean?"

"Well, you committed to the leadership team that you were going to hit the growth goals and rebound from last year's flat performance. What was the plan? What changes did you make in strategy, activity, or skills to make your team more effective and efficient than it was last year?"

There was a little silence.

Owen filled it by asking—politely and quietly—his next question. "You didn't add any staff, correct?"

"Yes, that's correct."

"So obviously, to increase results, it's only logical that effectiveness and efficiency would have to improve if you wanted to change the outcome, right?"

Tom squirmed in his chair a bit.

Owen let the silence continue, and watched dispassionately as Tom became even more uneasy. *Good*, Owen thought. *Phase 1 has begun: Afflict the comfortable! Later, when he starts to take action, I'll start putting him back together with Phase 2: Comfort the afflicted.*

Finally Tom broke the silence and said, "We didn't exactly do a sales plan. I figured the salespeople knew what to do, and they would step up and get it done."

"Hmm. Let's dive into that a little deeper. When you looked at the gap between last year's results and this year's goal, what were the changes to strategy that you identified?"

Tom shifted in his chair again. "Well," he said, "I told the sales staff that they needed to grow their territories by 18% across the board. That would more than cover our growth objectives. I also told them that we needed to consistently make our monthly numbers. Now, it's common knowledge that, in order to do that, they are going to have to bring in some new accounts."

"OK. I'm hearing a lot of emphasis on sales production, on targets that the sales team needs to meet. My question, though, is related to strategic changes you, yourself, have made—about what you've done to move the department in a new direction."

Tom stared at the ceiling for a long moment. When he looked at Owen and continued the conversation, there was a trace of defensiveness in his voice. "It's not like I'm ignoring my job. I'm requiring a weekly call report from each representative detailing the number of appointments they've set and the contact information for each, and I'm requiring them to give me in-depth notes about all new business opportunities. Honestly, though, a lot of what I get in those reports is smoke and fantasy. Here, let me show you."

Tom began to tap on the computer keys to call up the past week's reports, but Owen said, "That won't be necessary. I've seen this problem before. Tom, can I ask you a question?"

Tom stopped typing. "Sure," he said. But he was still staring at his computer screen. When he realized Owen was waiting for his full attention, he turned and looked at him.

"If a salesperson on your team is not successful, whose fault is it?"

Tom thought about that one for a moment. "Well," he said, "that depends."

Owen smiled. He recognized this as the response of a sales manager who is trying to come up with an answer to this tough question, but doesn't want to reply with the obvious—and correct—one.

Tom went on: "If the salesperson is brand-new to sales and the manager doesn't train him on the products and doesn't show him where to find business, then it's the manager's fault. But if the salesperson is experienced—and let's be honest here, just about everyone on my team is—then the salesperson has to own the failure."

"That's partially true, Tom. If an experienced person and a new hire are both given the tools to succeed, and both placed in an environment of growth and learning, they certainly should be expected to succeed. If they choose not to embrace the growth environment, then of course they will be responsible for their own downfall. Where I'm struggling, Tom, is that I'm not hearing that either the tools or the development opportunities are being provided. Can you see that that rests squarely on your shoulders?"

Tom shrugged, bowed his head, rubbed his eyes, and took a deep breath. He let out a deep sigh, and it was a little louder coming out than he'd meant it to be. He was glad this was a private meeting. When he looked up again, he saw Owen, still waiting for an answer. "Yes," Tom said, a little sheepishly. "When you put it that way, I can see what you mean."

"Don't feel bad about this, Tom. Many, many managers miss that concept. They overlook the reality that developing their people is a primary responsibility of their role. You've got that now. So let's keep moving—we've got a lot of work to do. We know now that the manager's role is to lead the people and manage the process. Too often, managers fall short of leading because they haven't set the course and haven't established trust among their people. Tom, can I ask you another tough question?"

"Sure."

"Can you see that your people might need to see a change in you before they can buy into the need to change what they're doing?"

Tom took another deep breath, nodded, and said, "Yes, I do—but I have absolutely no clue how to make that happen. I'm really going to need some help on that one if I'm going to do it."

Good, Owen thought. *He's opening up and taking responsibility.* "Now I need to ask you something else, Tom—are you sure you are personally committed to fix these problems?"

"Of course, I am," Tom said. "I'm hoping you've picked that much up from our conversations thus far."

"OK. And you want my help?"

"Definitely," Tom said. "I am going to need help. I realize that. Ultimately, this is my issue." There was no hesitation whatsoever in his voice.

Now we can get to work, Owen thought.

> **Big Ideas**
>
> - If you haven't already found one, find a coach. With their support, identify the true challenges you face. These should be your issues, not something that someone else is responsible for fixing.
> - You must be able to articulate each problem and the impact the problem is having on you or your department.
> - You must be personally committed to fix the problem.

Be Intentional about Humility

Throughout my career, I've had the opportunity to work alongside managers of differing levels of experience and success. I've asked myself, *What one trait do the most successful managers have in common?*

The most consistent thread I've seen with the most successful managers is what I like to call a "confident humility." These managers are lifelong learners. They never feel like they have arrived and no longer need to improve themselves; they are comfortable receiving constructive feedback from those they respect.

On the other end of the spectrum, I've seen managers who are in the early stages of their career and who act as if they have everything figured out. They simply will not admit to a mistake. They tend to be far less successful financially.

Put yourself in the shoes of an employee. Who would you rather work for? Who would you rather go to for encouragement? Who would you choose to keep working for? I believe most employees would prefer to sign on with the manager with confident humility. The likelihood of that manager listening, showing empathy, asking clarifying questions, and helping the salesperson move their career to the next level is much greater than the manager who is so insecure that they need to make the meeting all about them or put an employee down to make themselves feel better.

The moral here is a simple one: Admit it when you don't know something. Show a little vulnerability. Being intentional about humility as a manager builds trust, which in turn gives you the platform to build up your people.

Managers who are looking for change must start with themselves. It is your job to identify the direction in which your team must be led. If a change is required—and it usually is—you must identify the leadership skills and the overall strategy that must be in place in order to facilitate that change. If you are missing something important in terms of techniques (skills), in terms of daily behavior (execution), or in terms of attitude, you need to understand what those gaps are and seek out the best ways to fill them. It's highly likely that you, yourself, will need some coaching along the way. It is not weakness, but strength, to acknowledge this reality.

CHAPTER 7

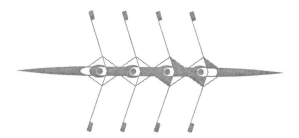

One-on-One

The next day, Tom arrived at his office early—seven o'clock. He was eager to get started, and he wanted to show Owen he was serious about understanding and fulfilling his role as a manager. More importantly, he wanted to demonstrate that he understood the need for change and that this change had to come from him first—as a leader.

By the time Owen arrived, at about eight, Tom had compiled revenues and margins by territory for the last three years. Tom couldn't wait to analyze the data and brainstorm with Owen about what the strategic plan should look like.

"It looks like you're all ready to get started," Owen said.

"Yes, I definitely am."

"Great! Why don't we start with you sharing what you think has to change, based on what we discussed yesterday."

"Good idea. First and foremost, the most critical change happens with me. I've got to drive the strategy toward incremental growth, and I have to wedge complacency, excuse-making, and status quo thinking out of our sales culture. I recognize that I created that, so it is clearly up to me to eliminate it."

Owen nodded and said, "OK. How do you plan to do that?"

"I'm not sure—but I'm open to suggestions."

Sensing an opening, Owen decided to make the most of it. "Leaders," he said, "have to show their commitment through their actions. All the slogans, speeches, and PowerPoints in the world will be overshadowed if the team doesn't see the leader going first."

"What are you saying, exactly, Owen? I was in here at seven o'clock this morning! Doesn't that prove I'm making a change? What am I supposed to do? Go out and find new accounts for my people?"

"No, of course not—though a lot of managers do make that very mistake. But, Tom, as the leader, you do have to provide the tools and the resources, as I mentioned earlier. That starts with improved communication between you and the team. Communication has many elements, including frequency, consistency, and clarity. Over time, if you pay attention to those three elements, you really can build trust—and trust is where you need to get with your people. Agreed?"

Tom nodded. "Agreed."

"Without trust, you can only try to lead. No one will actually follow. Most people want to trust their managers; often, they decide they can't because they've been let down by infrequent communication and inconsistency of expectations. This typically happens because of mixed messages, a lack of clear direction, or both. So I would suggest that, while it's great that you got in here early this morning, improving communication between management and staff is actually the right place to start. Doing only that much has had a major positive impact on most of the teams I've worked with."

"That makes sense," said Tom. "But where do I start?"

"I think what you'll find, Tom, is that it's an incremental process: as communication improves, the support and buy-in for the vision will also improve and then the communication will improve even more. But beginning the process of improving communication isn't easy. It takes work and practice. Many managers believe they communicate well when the reality is they pump out a lot of emails and memos and hold occasional group meetings that don't accomplish much. Let's start by remembering that the very best form of communication is still the one-on-one conversation—what you and I are doing right now. That's where real interaction can take place. That's where I would suggest you begin. Despite all the technological advances in communication we have at our disposal, the in-person, one-on-one conversation where both sides feel safe enough to share what's on their minds is still the best platform for connecting with team members."

"All true," said Tom. "Hearing you talk, I realize I haven't had enough of those one-on-one discussions lately. I'm thinking that may explain a lot about the last six months."

"How so?"

"Six months ago was when I was just beginning to feel the pressure from J.D., the numbers weren't coming in and I could sense his hesitation about my team's performance. Because of that, I was increasing my pressure on the team."

"Tell me more."

"I was checking on them multiple times per day, calling them in the field, demanding updates, and telling them to keep me in the loop about wins and losses."

"Hadn't they been doing that already?"

"Yes—but I guess I just wanted them to feel the same urgency that I was feeling about turning the numbers around."

"And what happened?"

Tom thought for a moment, and then said, "Nothing positive. The resentment began to build. I could sense from their messages that they were trying to keep their distance. When we did talk one-on-one, I found their answers cryptic, like they were trying to hold back information or limit the amount of detail they gave me. I realize now that I was the one who caused that because of my reaction to the pressure I was under. We weren't having discussions about strategies and tactics to increase business. It was more like I was conducting an interrogation, one that regularly ended with me telling them they needed to prospect more, present more, and close more. They probably got pretty sick of hearing it."

"Tom, did you ever talk about the gap between what you expected and what was happening?"

"Sure—every week at our sales meeting. I would review the numbers, highlight the territories that were the furthest behind, and ask for account updates on any customers that were behind last year's sales."

"How about during your one-on-one meetings?" Owen asked.

Tom looked puzzled. "You mean when I would check on a specific account or ask one of them directly for a territory update?"

"No, I mean when you met with a team member in private for a one-on-one coaching session."

"Oh," Tom said. "I didn't really do that. I wanted to maximize their selling time, so we just had the weekly group meetings. The rest of the time I wanted them out there selling."

"Tom, can you remind me again of how many salespeople report to you?"

"Five."

"OK. Do you think all five are faced with exactly the same challenges when it comes to reaching a higher level of performance?"

"Well—no, probably not."

"Then can I ask why you thought you could treat them all the same to improve their results?"

"I guess I figured if I said something enough times they would figure it out. They all have a decent amount of sales experience. If they needed something from me, they could always ask."

"Why do you suppose they didn't ask?"

Tom thought about that, and then said, "I probably didn't give them the environment they needed to ask for help—and you know what, as I'm saying it now, I realize I probably didn't give them much of a reason to trust me."

"Why do you say that, Tom?"

"As the numbers started to look bad and the business wasn't coming in, I knew all eyes were on the sales department. I started to distance myself from the salespeople, remove myself from their circle. I realize now that I created a gap between them and me. Them not turning to me must have been a survival or self-preservation thing. Surely they could all feel me holding them at arm's length—and I didn't give them much of a reason to trust me, much less work with me to turn things around."

Owen said, "Tom, I think you're making some important

discoveries about the relationships you damaged and the critical need to rebuild them. What do you think should happen now?"

"It's pretty obvious, I think. I need to let them know we are on the same side and we are in this together."

"OK. How are you planning to do that?"

"Hmm. I guess my first instinct would be to get them all together, tell them things have changed, and let them know that we need to work together as a team."

"Are you sure about that?"

Tom smiled. "I get it. Your advice would be to meet them one-on-one and begin to rebuild each relationship by meeting them where they are. Right?"

"I think you are on point," Owen said. "Would it help if we set aside time to talk about what that would sound like and the order of your meetings?"

"Sure."

"Why don't we break for today and meet again tomorrow morning? Maybe when we talk next, we could start with you telling me about each of the salespeople and their role on the team. Then we can plan the meetings from there."

"I can do that," Tom said. "I need to get through a bunch of emails, so stopping now sounds good."

"It's a plan," Owen said. "I'll see you tomorrow."

Big Ideas

- The very best form of communication is still the one-on-one conversation. That's where real interaction can take place.
- Different salespeople face different performance challenges. Don't expect to be able to help them by sharing the same guidance with all of them.
- Take the time to understand each salesperson as an individual.

Be Intentional about Strategy

Strategy is an intentional act of looking at a situation from a new perspective and determining if things have changed or are changing. Managers often become managers because they were doers as salespeople. The thought of stopping to analyze and possibly change course feels unproductive.

Many salespeople have this same thought: "If I just do more, the results will come." Sometimes this approach works when you're a salesperson, but being in management requires a deeper commitment. The business landscape is dynamic and ever changing. To thrive, a manager must step out of daily business and determine whether adjustments are required in the plan, offering, or approach—and, if so, what those adjustments might be. It is then incumbent upon the manager to redirect the salespeople if a change is required and to ensure they have the skills and tools to execute the new strategy.

CHAPTER 8

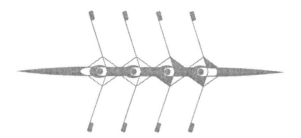

Goal Time vs. Clock Time

Owen walked into Tom's office at the agreed-upon time the next morning, eight o'clock. Tom was sitting proudly behind his desk, working on his second cup of coffee. Stacks of account files for each of his sales representatives lay before him.

Owen asked, "What's with all the files?"

Tom replied, "I thought we would go through these files to uncover where each of the reps needs help to make their quota. Then I could tell them where they should go and who they should talk to in order to get their numbers up."

Owen looked quizzical, and Tom had an immediate sense

that he had taken a wrong turn. "Tom, haven't you been 'telling them' for the last six months?"

"Yes—but sometimes this particular tactic has worked."

"That's good to know, because our aim is to make you an intentional sales manager. We do want to figure out what has worked, and is working, for each individual salesperson. But that's not necessarily where we want to start."

"What do you mean?"

"Tom, you're leaping ahead to the tactics, the behaviors. We have to look at the attitudes first. We want you to lead each of your people to help them identify the key activities that they must achieve daily, weekly, or monthly in order for them to maximize their performance. Then, we want them to be motivated to execute those behaviors consistently and to do so using the most efficient schedule possible. This is what we call working on 'goal time,' not clock time. To make the most of goal time, we have to harness the purpose of the individual salesperson—their own personal sense of immediacy and urgency. Make sense?"

Tom nodded. He thought back on the many times he had noted a lack of urgency on his team.

"You see," Owen continued, "many managers emphasize working hard as a key to success. Yet, don't we see countless examples of underperforming salespeople putting in long

Goal Time vs. Clock Time

hours—what we call 'clock time'—and then becoming frustrated with low sales results?"

"Sure."

"What happens next? Typically, the manager puts pressure on the salesperson to work even harder, but the results don't change because the salesperson has lost confidence. A negative self-perpetuating cycle sets in: 'I work harder; I don't get the results I want; I wonder if I'm any good at this.' It's a continuous feedback loop of doubt, concern, pressure, and failure. So if you agree, Tom, let's talk about getting all this started with your people. Let's start with purpose. Now, do you think we should start with your top producer or your hardest worker?"

"I'm thinking my hardest worker. That would be Jason. He works hard every day. However, I'm not sure I see the results in his sales production."

"Hmm. Would it make sense for us to start with me asking you to answer the questions in a format that you would ask Jason? That way you would have a feel for the conversation from the salesperson's perspective."

"That would be great."

"OK. You could start by asking Jason, 'Why do you work the way you do?' What do you think he'd say in response, Tom?"

This gave Tom pause. He was expecting a straightforward role-play, not a question like this. "Well," he said finally, "I'm only guessing, but maybe it's how he was raised—or somebody told him to always work hard." Tom shrugged his shoulders.

"It seems like you answered the question of how he works. What if you were to focus on the *why* in the question? Listen as I ask it again, generally: 'Why do you work the way you do?'"

"Ah. I heard it that time."

"What did you hear?"

"I'm trying to understand the underlying purpose behind their work."

"Exactly. As an intentional sales manager, you are helping them to understand their *why*—which is much deeper than the question of what someone does or even how someone does it. The recognition of *why* between you and the salesperson begins the process of setting goals. It also helps to build trust, which you will need as you begin to hold them accountable."

"I see."

"Tom, true motivation is always anchored in an individual's *why*. That *why* is sometimes readily apparent, but it is usually a good deal harder to access. We can't assume we know what it is. Very often, the individual isn't fully aware of their own *why*."

"That's where we come in?"

"You've got it. As intentional sales managers, we help them realize their *why*, which results in them setting goals and staying focused. So, should we talk about the next question?"

"Sure," Tom said.

"Next, you could ask Jason: 'What do you want to achieve?'"

"That's easy. I know what he'll say. To make quota consistently and earn a good living, just like everyone else."

Owen smiled. "I'm sure that's part of it," he said. "But that second question is meant to illuminate both the short and the long term. Making quota may address short-term goals, but long term, he may want a promotion, or he may want to run his own company, or he may want to be recognized as an industry leader. We just don't know."

"I see what you mean."

"Your role as a leader is to help him align his work with his long-term vision and design a belief system that supports it. You see, some people actually do have a vision for the future, and they may even have goals. But if their beliefs don't support the vision, they can subconsciously sabotage the vision for the simple reason that they don't believe it's possible. At some level, deep down, they don't think they deserve to be that person in the future state."

"That makes sense," Tom said. "That would be why I see repetitive patterns of mediocrity or stagnation."

"You've got it."

"Now that I think of it, I can even recall a number of occasions where one of my underperforming salespeople had a killer quarter, only to figure out a way to miss quota in the following quarters, resulting in a typical inferior performance for the year."

"Yep, that happens."

"Let me guess. The next question asks them how."

"You're on it," Owen said. "It sounds like this: 'How do you need to change to achieve your goals in the future state?'"

"OK," Tom said. "I see we are finally on to the tactical part of the process, where we are identifying the action items."

"Yes, but don't miss the nuance of the question. First, note that the question has them recognize that to have a different outcome, the input needs to change. We've all heard the practical definition of insanity, right?"

"Yes—doing the same thing over and over and expecting a different result."

"You got it," Owen said. "Here's a fun fact. Albert Einstein is often credited with that axiom. Yet he himself said, 'I probably didn't say that!' But it is certainly said on a regular basis, and it's a concept that we should all know. Wouldn't you agree?"

"Sure."

"We often need others to point it out to us when we are caught up in an unhealthy routine. There's a little coaching trick for you, by the way. That saying may come in handy at some point in your discussions with your people." Owen smiled, then said, "To move on: The other part of the question that should not be missed is the emphasis on 'you' and 'your.' What I want you to notice is that this is a reinforcement of the salesperson taking personal ownership of the act of changing habits, as part of the effort to accomplish goals."

"I'm tracking with you. What else should come from this question?"

"As you mentioned, it brings out the tactical application of the deliverable. We can think of these three questions as covering all elements of success: the behaviors, activities, and tasks coupled with the attitude, mindset, and outlook. They all have to work together, don't they?"

"I guess so. Can you give me an example of what you mean?"

"Sure. Let's say Jason wants to get better at asking for referrals. He needs to commit to a certain number of activities to get a certain number of referrals on a weekly basis. But that's not enough, is it? He also has to believe that asking for referrals is appropriate and important. With those two elements in place, he can execute the specific techniques to successfully generate referrals—assuming, of course, that he possesses the skills in question. The absence of any one of these elements leaves the outcome subject to random chance."

"I see. It's like a puzzle with three pieces. They've all got to be there: the skills, the day-to-day behaviors, and the attitude."

"Exactly. Now, Tom, at the risk of stating the obvious, your salespeople each have a different *why*. That means each requires unique goals and plans. As you operate as an intentional motivator, you will help facilitate their personal discoveries, help them design their plans, and help them learn to hold themselves accountable for achieving success as they've defined it. The critical role you play is in being consistent with each person, tracking their progress, and providing resources—or being a resource—when they get stuck."

"Makes sense," said Tom, nodding. "I have to say, this is nothing like the way I was managing before."

Just then, J.D. knocked on the open door. "Hey—you guys making progress?"

Owen looked at Tom and waited for him to reply.

"Well," Tom said, "we have definitely identified the root cause of the sales department's problems."

"And?"

"And..." Tom hesitated, but decided he had to admit it—even to his own boss. "It's me. It's the way that I was focusing on the results, or the lack thereof. It's me not providing resources for my team to be successful. Owen has helped me realize that my team is made up of individuals with different reasons for coming to work, and if they are ever to reach their full potential, I'm the wild card that can increase or decrease the odds of that happening."

"Congratulations! Sounds right," J.D. said.

Tom breathed a sigh of relief.

J.D. continued, "So, what's next?"

Owen jumped in. "We haven't gotten to the specifics yet, but Tom will need to meet with each of his people for a goals discussion, which will result in a behavior plan that he will use to hold them accountable. During the plan creation and their weekly individual meetings, they will uncover areas that need development. When that occurs, Tom will be documenting an individual training plan that will be tracked at future meetings."

Tom's head spun a little at all this, but it sounded like it would all be helpful.

"OK," J.D. said. "Sounds like you guys have turned a corner. Keep me posted, Tom."

"Will do," Tom said. As J.D. disappeared down the hall, Tom noticed a little smile on Owen's face.

"So," Owen said, his face suddenly all business once again, "are you ready to meet the salespeople?"

"Yep—can't wait."

"Here's what I suggest. Plan on the introduction to the whole process to be a two-part meeting. The first will explain the goal process. The second, which you'll hold a few days later, will review and refine the goals that they come back to you with. During that second meeting, you'll co-create a behavioral plan. Once that is set up, you will need to establish a weekly cadence of individual meetings to review their progress. I can help you with that. What do you think?"

"Sounds good," Tom said.

Owen said, "Why don't you and I plan to talk by phone tomorrow morning, and then meet two weeks from today. We can review the progress then, and address the additional leadership elements that will help you become a truly intentional sales manager. Sound good?"

"Sounds great," said Tom. "Looking forward to it. In the meantime, I'll get started planning those one-on-one discussions with my team members."

Big Ideas

- In evaluating the members of your sales team, look first at attitude.
- True motivation is always anchored in an individual's *why*. That *why* is sometimes readily apparent, but it is often difficult to access. You can't assume you know what it is.
- Essential questions to ask salespeople during one-on-one meetings include: "Why do you work the way you do?" "What do you want to achieve?" "How do you need to change to achieve your goals in the future state?"

Be Intentional about Goals and Goal Facilitation

"Goal time" is working with intention on things that align with your goals and activities that will move you toward the achievement of your goals. These activities are often measurable and quantifiable. The concept of goal time starts with a plan and a series of actions that will achieve that plan. Once all the actions are complete, we have the option to go do whatever activity we enjoy doing that is in line with the plan and supports the goals.

Goal time stands in contrast to clock time. In clock time, you stay busy doing activities that seem like they are productive but are not moving you measurably closer to the goal achievement. Why does anyone spend so much of their day in clock time? Because doing so matches up with how the human brain works. People will often do things that are non-threatening or comfortable, until their reticular activating system — a diffuse network of nerve pathways that mediates human consciousness — kicks in and prompts them to do something different. This new action comes from a different part of the brain and requires conscious thought. Those thoughts are a result of intentional plans that have not only been identified but have been seen as personally compelling.

Much like a business creates a vision for its future and uses it as a focal point for the whole organization, an individual must have a personal vision for what they want to achieve and be intentional about their daily activities to ensure that they are working toward the vision. All the elements of corporate goal setting apply to individual goal setting. There must be an established and embraced goal, a plan to achieve it, documented elements of a compelling plan, and a process in place to measure the progress. Individuals will often commit to a goal in their head but resist the planning and documentation elements. In the absence of a stated and documented individual goal, the human brain will default to its primal instinct—specifically, fear—when faced with the challenges of achieving new levels of performance, mainly because it's unchartered territory. When you do something new and potentially scary for the first time, be it jump off a diving board, speak in public, or call a big prospective customer, your drive to do so must be activated by your post-primal brain, which depends on the steps of documenting and measuring our activities. An understanding of these principles is essential to individual goal facilitation, which is an essential part of your job as an intentional sales manager.

Individual goal facilitation is all too often the forgotten element in the manager's effort to develop their people. The focus is generally on the needs of the business, and they assume that the salesperson will make the connection that if the business or department is successful, they will be successful. In fact, managers have to help them connect the dots. True motivation is only in place when an individual employee has concrete reasons to conclude that what is good for the company is equally good for them. These reasons are unique to each individual. It is your job as a manager to help salespeople find these reasons and internalize them. This breeds loyalty, trust, and perseverance.

CHAPTER 9

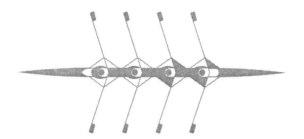

The Attitude Shift

Tom and Owen had agreed to meet at the Crossroads Diner. It was a Saturday morning so the place wasn't as crowded as it was during the work week. As usual, Sam, the owner, was there, seating the customers and talking up the specials.

"Hey there," Sam said, when she saw Tom and Owen. "Welcome back to the Crossroads, gents. A pleasant surprise! Not used to seeing you here on a Saturday, Tom!"

"Sam, I guess it's the new me," Tom said. "These are planning meetings with my buddy Owen here. I've got a vision for where we can take the business, and I've got to be a better resource for my people if I want to get there and build a self-sufficient team. This meeting is all about figuring that part out."

"We're sure glad to have you back," said Sam, showing them to a table. Then she made her way to some other customers who were looking to be served. The aromas of bacon, eggs, and coffee mixed together into a heady, fresh smell that said, "This brand new day is officially underway."

After they'd ordered, Tom turned to Owen and said, "Ready to get down to business?"

Owen nodded. "Looks like you showed up ready to work," he said, pointing at Tom's three-inch binder, neatly arranged with colored tabs indicating each salesperson's section.

"Yeah. I thought this would be a good way to document my individual meetings—and subtly remind myself that I'm changing while I'm asking the salespeople to change. Here, let me show you." He reached for the book, placed it on the counter, and turned it toward Owen.

Owen put his hand on the binder, preventing Tom from opening it. "Maybe that can wait," Owen said. "Why don't you start by telling me about what you remember most about your conversations? Then you can check the notes and see what you might have missed. It's a good way to strengthen your memory about individual salespeople and their issues."

"Oh—OK. As agreed, I started with Jason. You'll remember he's been with us for just over a year, and he's probably my hardest worker. Knowing that our department was under the microscope, he was rather anxious in our meeting. I'd scheduled it for late in the day so I guess he associated that with big trouble. The minute I sat down across the desk from him, I could tell he thought he was about to be let go. I have to admit, it surprised me to see that his trust in me had sunk so low that he thought he was going to be fired without warning."

"What did you do?" asked Owen.

"I could see how concerned he was. I immediately addressed his concern by telling him that he had nothing to worry about."

"Great. And how did that go over?"

"Really well. He was relieved."

"Then what happened?"

"I explained to him about the work you and I have been doing and apologized that I had not been providing the support and direction that a manager should. I made a commitment to him that that would change, starting now."

"And how did he respond to that?"

"It was amazing. A total attitude shift. That one simple promise from my side took every bit of discomfort out of the room. It was like I had punched a reset button on our whole working relationship."

"I'm not surprised," Owen said. "Making an open admission like that, without strings or qualifications, is a great way to get team members feeling OK about the relationship. That kind of promise ends the blame game. Well done! How did you proceed from there?"

"Can I check my notes now?"

"Sure."

Tom opened the binder and briefly reviewed his notes on his conversation with Jason. "Pretty early in the conversation Jason had gone from being concerned to just being curious about what was going on," he said. "After a few moments, he grasped the purpose of the meeting and started to show some optimism. I asked him the questions you shared with me, in the same order. 'Why do you work the way you do?' 'What do you want to achieve?' 'How do you need to change to achieve your goals in the future state?'

"Unlike the way I at first heard the question when you asked me, though, Jason picked right up on the intention of what I was asking. He was able to articulate his personal vision of the future and share why he worked the way he did.

"He said he considered his coworkers to be something very close to family. I asked a couple of questions about that, and I found out that Jason comes from a family where hard work was instilled in everyone at a young age. He laughed when he thought about how his father worked so hard on projects around the house that could have been accomplished much easier or quicker if he had just taken the time to consider his options or apply the right tools. With a little coaxing and some more discussion, I was able to get Jason to start reflecting on his professional and family goals."

"Did he share any of those goals with you?"

"No, but he said he would give them some more thought and get back to me by the end of next week with a written list."

Owen nodded but said nothing, as though to encourage Tom to complete the thought he had just started.

"Hey," Tom said. "What if he doesn't do what he committed to do?"

"Good question," said Owen. He smiled and waited for Tom to keep going.

"In the past, I would just accept the excuses and give him a couple more days."

"Is that the best way forward now, do you think?"

"Maybe not. Can you give me a hint as to what you think I should be doing if he doesn't follow through?"

Owen leaned forward. "Here are a couple of things to consider. First, this is for his benefit so the odds are greater than before that he will want to make it a priority. Second, I might suggest that you ask him for a status report a couple of days before the deadline. Regardless of what he tells you in response to that, I would remind him of the deadline that he committed to. If he doesn't deliver it as promised, I would suggest that you meet with him in person and review your agreements with each other and the importance of meeting commitments going forward—being sure to do this as a peer, not as someone who's criticizing him or judging him. Does that make sense?"

"Absolutely."

"Great. Who did you talk to next?"

"Camila," said Tom. "That was a very interesting meeting."

> **Big Ideas**
>
> - Be personally committed to becoming a better resource for your people.
> - Making an open, unqualified admission of having failed to live up to a commitment is a great way to get team members feeling OK about their relationship with you.
> - When a salesperson makes a commitment to do something important by a certain date, consider sharing a tactful, drama-free reminder of the commitment a couple of days before the deadline.

Be Intentional about Organization

Truly intentional sales management requires a different level of organization than the role of salesperson, which is the professional role that most managers played previously. As the manager, it's extremely important that you carefully document activities, commitments, and items for follow up. Very often, the salesperson's success depends on your ability to hold them accountable for specific commitments. With multiple people on your team, it's difficult to do this well without an effective organizational system.

Contrary to what managers may wish to believe, staff will always notice if their manager isn't organized. They will very soon thereafter either resent whatever time they spend with a disorganized manager or find a way to use the manager's disorganization to avoid being held accountable. Being well organized helps you run an efficient department, allowing you to find a balance between tasks and strategies and avoid being caught in administrative quicksand.

CHAPTER 10

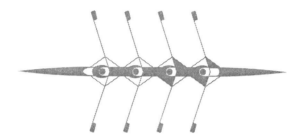

The Antidote to Paranoia

Sam poured their coffee refills as Tom and Owen continued their breakfast.

"As I said," Tom said, "the next meeting I had scheduled was with Camila. Based on what I'd learned during my meeting with Jason, I figured that she would probably not be able to focus until she knew why I was scheduling one-on-one meetings. It was not part of the routine that I would meet privately with her. In addition, my own assessment was that she was the most paranoid of the bunch."

"What makes you say that?" Owen asked.

"Well, Camila's numbers are consistently low and have been for some time, and I suspect, when I scheduled a meeting with her, that she, too, figured her days were numbered."

"Yes, that can be a recurring problem with these meetings the first time around. I'm sorry I didn't warn you about that."

"No, I probably should have figured it out on my own and said something ahead of time to prepare her. Honestly, though if it wasn't so sad it would have been funny."

"What do you mean?"

"Before I could even start the meeting, she came up with excuses backed up by more excuses, backed up by still more excuses. I heard about two dozen different reasons why various deals hadn't come through. She was totally committed to controlling this conversation—which maybe is how she's been running her meetings with prospects."

"It's a possibility," said Owen.

"There came a point where I had to raise my hand and surrender, just to get her to stop talking. I said, 'Camila, let's start over. I didn't call this meeting to fire you. I guess I need to explain the purpose of this meeting and what I'm intending to do going forward.'"

"How did she react to that?"

"She seemed a little taken aback; I don't think she understood what I was saying beyond, 'I didn't call this meeting to fire you.' When I went on to say that I was the one at fault for the culture in the department and that I knew things had to change, she sat back in her chair and released the death grip she had on the corner of my desk."

"Good sign!"

"Yes. I thought so, too. I went on to explain the process and plan I was looking to put in place for each salesperson, with the aim of being a resource to meet their goals. I told her I was committed to seeing things from a different perspective—her perspective."

"What happened then?"

"Initially, she saw this as an opportunity to place her lack of production at the foot of the 'blame the manager' altar. Once I had redirected her thinking, though, by explaining that the new approach I was after was based on collaboration and a commitment to her personal growth, I began to share the questions that we needed to explore together: 'Why do you work the way you do?' 'What do you want to achieve?' 'How do you need to change to achieve your goals in the future state?'

"As the questions began to sink in, I don't know which of us was more surprised—Camila or me. She had recognized a shift in culture toward individual accountability, and I could tell she was beginning to take it seriously. For my part, I realized that these concepts and questions had never crossed Camila's mind. She had made a career, and maybe even a lifetime, out of blaming others and playing the part of the victim. I could see now that she was exploring another possibility."

"So what happened next?"

"Given how far she had to go, I decided to suggest that she start small and identify one personal and one professional goal that she would like to achieve within the next 60 days. We are scheduled to meet next Wednesday to discuss what she decided and to create a plan to accomplish those two goals. She agreed to get those to me in writing by the end of the day tomorrow. The accelerated timing was her idea, which I see as a good sign. I'll find a way to mention that timing to her today, just as a subtle reminder of what we'd agreed to. Then when she does pass along the list, I'll be sure to give her a high five."

"Great idea," said Owen. "It's important for people to see success early on, especially if they are not in the habit of setting goals. You've laid the groundwork well, Tom—and you have changed the dynamic in the relationship. Hopefully, the paranoia phase has passed. Now the real work can begin. Once you have gotten some clarity on Camila's personal goals, you can start the process of tying those personal goals to specific performance targets."

> **Big Ideas**
>
> - Have an in-depth one-on-one discussion with each salesperson about their *why* and develop personal goals based on that *why*.
> - Help people to experience small wins early on, especially if they are not in the habit of setting and taking action on goals.

Be Intentional about Tying Performance Targets to Goals

Personal goals act as the fuel to professional goals and success. Once the individual can activate the powers of the subconscious mind in support of personal goal achievement, they begin to realize the connection between professional goal success and their own world.

A big part of the intentional sales manager's job is to answer the primal-instinct question, "What's in it for me?" Help the salesperson identify what aspect of their life they would like to positively impact, and then help them to connect specific workplace behaviors to the improvement of those areas of life.

While the process is different for everyone, the most important personal priorities tend to show up in categories like finances, family, career, social connection, and health. Once objectives in those areas are identified and documented, you can then help the employee by making and consistently reinforcing the connection between the company or department goals and the employee's personal goals. This must take place in a private, one-on-one meeting in which the salesperson feels safe. Only as a result of such discussions can the employee begin to experience, on an emotional level, the correlation between company success and (for instance) their once-in-a-lifetime family vacation.

This connection of personal goals to work performance does not come naturally for most employees. They don't do it on their own, and you can't expect them to. Instead, consistently, tactfully, and patiently remind them that work achievement is a means to the achievement of important personal goals. When more prospecting becomes the same as funding that dream vacation, it will become a priority.

CHAPTER 11

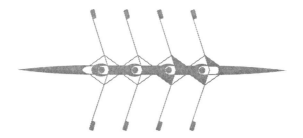

The Breakthrough

As Owen poured syrup on his pancakes at the diner, he asked Tom, "Who did you talk to next?"

"My next meeting," Tom said, "was with Keiko, our top producer. I wasn't sure what to expect given her usual response to my attempts to manage her."

"What do you mean?"

"She always seems to look for special treatment or dispensation related to policies, rules, or standards because she earns the most. Regardless of the topic, Keiko looks for a reason that she shouldn't have to comply with the same rules that everyone else does. I recognize that she contributes a great deal to the overall department numbers, but I still don't think she is reaching her potential. Of course, I can't afford to lose her so it's always been an awkward situation when she pushes back. I find myself compromising or conceding and giving her a pass. If her production were to ever start to slip, I've got a feeling she would move on to another company before her earnings—and her ego—took a hit."

"So that's the background—got it. How did the meeting go?"

"I'm happy to say that it went much better this time. I started acknowledging to Keiko that my management decisions had been holding her back and not helping her to be even more successful. Suddenly I had her full attention!"

"That's a great way to reconnect with high performers and make them feel OK. Well done!"

"Then I went on to compliment her on her steady production, and I acknowledged that she was my top salesperson. I further explained that, from this point forward, I was going to help the other members of the team to set goals, be a resource for them, and hold them accountable to be intentionally successful."

"What did she have to say to that?"

"At that point, Keiko's smile turned to a look of concern. I wasn't quite sure what was going on, but then I heard words that were music to my ears."

Owen looked interested. "What words were those?" he asked.

"She said, 'What about me? I want to set goals and have you as a resource, too.' At which point I said, 'But you haven't wanted that in the past. Why now?'"

"And what did she have to say to that?"

"I couldn't believe it. She said, 'Tom, it wasn't because I didn't want it. You just weren't making me. What I know about myself is that I sometimes need to be pushed a little bit.'"

"Wow," said Owen. A broad grin spread across his face.

"I know. My guess is that she was afraid this new normal might just work, and that before long she would see her counterparts improving and their sales results increasing. At that point she might not be number one, or at least not the automatic number one."

"Fascinating. What happened next?"

"I went on to ask her the three critical questions you suggested: 'Why do you work the way you do?' 'What do you want to achieve?' 'How do you need to change to achieve your goals in the future state?'"

"And?"

"For the first time ever, I realized how self-aware Keiko was. She immediately honed in on the first question and explained that she was the first born of a family with five children. She had always performed well in school, on her soccer team, and in her attempts to play a musical instrument. She went on and on about this! She explained that this was not because she cared that much about grades or winning soccer games or playing the piano, but because she really cared how people would see her."

"That's remarkable. She really opened up!"

"It was those three questions, really. I could tell that they got her thinking. I remember specifically that she said, 'For the first time in my career, I realize that I work at being the top performer, not for personal satisfaction, but in order to look good to others. That's what drives me.'"

"Well done, sir!"

"It was a great moment for both of us, Owen. I then asked her what she most wanted to achieve, and she responded that she wanted to be passionate about her work."

"Anything else?"

"She said that if I could help her find that passion, I would never, ever have to worry about her sales performance. So for the next 30 minutes, I asked her more questions about why she did the things she did, both positive and negative. Keiko was amazingly transparent, which I believe surprised even her."

"So was that the end of the meeting?"

"Not even close. Keiko was just getting started. After we talked in depth about why she did the things she did and she'd opened up enough to examine both the admirable and the not-so-admirable implications of her behavior, the most remarkable thing of all happened."

"What was that?"

The Breakthrough

"She started talking, with real passion and conviction, about what she wanted to make happen in her life."

"That must have been powerful."

"It was," Tom said. "Before I even realized it, we had transitioned to an in-depth discussion about her personal goals. She started to get excited and actually stood up to pace around in my office. She described her desire to help children of single mothers, her dream house, and her need to save for retirement. When we were through, she agreed that the next step was for her to take some time to reflect even more on her goals, both personal and professional. She agreed to create a detailed written list of goals in the areas of social connection, family, education, finance, career, spirituality, and health."

"Sounds like you hit pay dirt. What was the agreed-upon next step?"

"We are scheduled to meet for 30 minutes next Friday to review her progress and discuss her plan—and also take a close look at the resources she will need to achieve her future state."

"Remarkable. That sounds like a breakthrough meeting for both of you. I'm really happy to hear how well that went, Tom."

"Me, too."

"Who else did you meet with?"

Tom smiled.

Big Ideas

- Most high performers are ready and willing to focus on things that will help them to move their career to the next level.
- If possible, coach high performers to create written goals in the following categories: social connection, family, education, finance, career, spirituality, and health.

Be Intentional about Perseverance

No two salespeople are alike. At the same time, everyone who reports to you needs some level of accountability and structure if they are going to achieve their true potential. As a manager, you need to understand that some employees will gravitate toward accountability and structure while others will initially resist. The most effective managers are able to persevere through the resistance by recognizing that resistance is part of the human condition.

People may have come to believe that being held accountable somehow limits their self-determination so their first instinct may be to fight the very notion of accountability and to dismiss all talk of workplace commitment as "micro management" or "babysitting." Yet once you find the right balance and the right emphasis for that specific person, you may see a breakthrough. Once people embrace the concept and are held accountable to the things that are truly important to them, they hold themselves accountable—and achieve far more.

CHAPTER 12

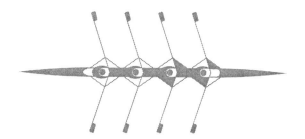

The Question of Questions

No one loved the bacon at Crossroads more than Tom, and he took a fortifying bite before continuing. "My next scheduled meeting," he then told Owen, "was with Stace. I learned something extremely important about her."

"What was that?" Owen asked.

"You may recall that she's my new hire—been out of college for only a couple of years. As I spoke with her, I picked up on one of her big challenges during meetings with prospects."

"Go on."

"Before our meeting, I found out Stace had asked around,

hoping to find out the purpose of the meeting from the other sales reps. She didn't get any useful background, though, because I'd asked all the team members to keep the proceedings private."

"OK."

"So when Stace came to my office, I asked, 'Do you know what the purpose of this meeting is?' I was curious to see what kind of response I'd get."

"What happened?"

"I was hoping for an open acknowledgement that Stace wasn't sure what the purpose was and a question from her that would help us to get the conversation started. But she didn't ask a question. She immediately started guessing based on what she thought she knew. At that moment, I realized that this was exactly the same problem she has on a sales call. Rather than simply asking for information, she takes a guess!"

"Good to know!"

"Anyway, after she had exhausted her list of reasons that she thought I wanted to hear, most of which had to do with salary reviews, I was finally able to explain what I was actually looking to accomplish. I told her about my goals for the meeting and my own recognition of the need for a change in my approach."

"How did she respond to that?"

"She seemed relieved to have an explanation, but she still didn't bother to pose a single question. We were now ten minutes or so into the discussion, and she hadn't asked me anything. I then told her we would be spending most of the session discussing her and that she would be doing most of the talking. At that point, a look of concern passed over her face. As I asked the first of the three questions ('Why do you work the way you do?'), she began to shift in her chair uneasily and show a look of bewilderment. There was a long pause. Finally, I asked if there was something wrong."

"What did she say?"

"A little sheepishly, she responded, 'I didn't know that was what you were going to ask.' Now I was the one who was confused! Stace went on to explain that she didn't know the right answer to my question—and she actually asked me to let her know what the right answer was! She wanted me to tell her why she worked the way she did."

"Wow! That's a first."

"It sure was. I saw that she was deeply uncomfortable saying something that might be perceived as wrong. It occurred to me that Stace had developed a zero-risk approach to life, one that prevented her from doing anything that could conceivably look like failure. That gave me pause."

Owen nodded and said, "So you see that as a problem?"

Tom's response was instant. "Absolutely!"

"Tell me why."

"Frankly, I'm horrified to think that I've got a salesperson on the payroll who won't ask a question, can't take a risk, and is afraid of failure. After all, this job is all about putting yourself out there. If you're guessing instead of asking, if you're afraid to fail, if you're afraid to take any risks, you aren't going to be very happy in this role."

"I understand—and I agree. So where did you leave things with Stace?"

"I gave her some short audio programs on setting goals and risk-taking, asked her to give them a listen, and then asked her to check back in with me on Friday to share what she'd learned from them."

Owen was unwilling to let that be the last word on the subject of Stace. "Just out of curiosity, what else is supposed to happen when you talk to her on Friday?"

"I figure I'll use that learning—or lack of it—as the foundation for a larger discussion about going outside the comfort zone, and see how Stace responds to that conversation," Tom responded. "If she's still stuck in 'please the teacher' mode, which is where I realize that she's been for the last six months, I think I'm going to have to start thinking about whether it really makes sense for her to keep working on my team. If I figure out on Friday that she's unlikely to ever make that transition out of 'don't take a chance,' then it doesn't make a lot of sense to start talking about a goals and accountability plan. On the other hand, if she's ready to move beyond the safety net, then

The Question of Questions

we can start building the plan together. What do you think of that approach?"

Owen nodded. "Sounds like exactly what I would do," he said.

> **Big Ideas**
>
> - The willingness and ability to ask a question, instead of just taking a guess about what's happening, is essential to the salesperson's role.
> - Strong aversion to any form of risk may signal that the person in question is not an ideal candidate for a sales job.
> - True success in sales—or in any field—requires being willing, on occasion, to go outside your comfort zone.

Be Intentional about Asking

A salesperson's single greatest tool is the question. Countless books and articles have been written about the astonishing power of questions during interactions with prospective buyers. Sales workshops focus on the importance of asking effective questions during a sales call, and many managers complain to me that their people don't ask enough questions. Managers spend all kinds of time going over the questions they want their salespeople to ask, but the salespeople somehow forget it all when they are in front of a prospect or in a selling situation. What is going on here? All it seems to take is an open-ended question from a prospect or something else that the salesperson hears as a so-called "buying signal," and salespeople throw away the plan. They stop asking questions and dive head first into telling mode.

This problem seems to be universal across industries and levels of experience. The best theory about why it happens is that at some point the salesperson presumes they know where the conversation is going, and they start making assumptions—committing what I like to call "assumicide." Perhaps the salesperson wants to display their industry knowledge and experience so they simply guess at the real question or the reason behind the question. Or maybe the salesperson wants to cut to the close so they fill in the blanks in their mind or justify that they can get the answers later.

Managers can help turn this extremely common cycle around by becoming intentional about their own questions and observing the "ask, don't tell" rule in their own interactions with members of the team.

One particularly critical behavior or habit is for managers to create a pattern of consistent, hard-hitting questions that are always used during debrief situations—questions that salespeople come to expect after discussions with prospective buyers and know they must be ready to answer intelligently.

Note that the most common opening question managers ask in these discussions—"How did it go?"—is useless. This question only elicits a subjective response, and delays the manager's ability to get a clear picture of the viable sales opportunity.

Examples of stronger questions would be:

"Why did the prospect say they needed our product or service?"

"Why did they agree to meet with you?"

> "Why are they looking to make a change?"
>
> Asking these questions consistently after each sales call conditions salespeople to pose more effective questions during their meetings, shows you how far along in the sales process they really are with a given opportunity, gives you a more aligned sales team, and helps you to more quickly identify areas where specific individuals may need training and development.

CHAPTER 13

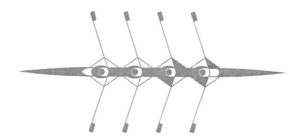

"I Want to Be You"

Tom and Owen were finishing up their last bites of their delicious breakfast as Tom said, "I only had one salesperson left—Ryan, my most senior performer. I believed he had the most to gain from this process, given his ample experience and his history of loyalty to the company. I felt I had to paint the whole picture for him, and give him a very clear sense of what was going on, before I asked him those three questions."

"Good idea," Owen said. "So how did you start the meeting?"

"I went through the plan. I explained that the sales department as a whole was still lagging behind in its commitments, while Finance and Operations were each on track to perform according to budget or better. I could see the look of concern in his eyes when I said that."

"Then what happened?"

"He asked what he could do to help. With Ryan, it was less about missing the numbers and more about letting other people down. Ryan looked at his coworkers—and at me—as family. He had always been quick to lend others a hand, and that's what he wanted to do now. But helping others was the last thing I needed from him. It was a delicate topic, because I knew I needed to help him recognize that the best way for him to help was for him to focus on his own sales responsibilities."

"Did you say that to him?"

"I did. I told him that it was extremely important now, if we were going to meet our commitments, that he not dilute his efforts by volunteering in other departments and taking on other people's problems as his own. I told him that, even though he probably knew how to resolve their issues, my request was that he leave the coaching to me and focus on his own daily accountabilities."

"And how did Ryan react to that?"

"He thought about it for a moment. Then he nodded, kind of solemn, and agreed to make that commitment to me. I could tell that he meant it."

"Then what happened?"

"From there I transitioned to the three questions, which

by now were pretty much second nature to me. Ryan's replies didn't surprise me. When I asked, 'Why do you work the way you do?' Ryan said that it was out of loyalty to his coworkers. In fact, he said this with such conviction that, in the pause that followed, I felt as though that was the only answer anyone could give. It was quite a moment."

"How about the second question?"

"When I asked Ryan what he wanted to achieve, he told me the main thing he wanted to achieve was the company mission. There wasn't a trace of irony or sarcasm in that statement; again, he really meant it. I smiled and acknowledged his commitment to his peers, to me, and to the company—and then I asked him to reflect on that question from a personal perspective. After staring at the ceiling for what seemed like ten or fifteen minutes, but was probably only one or two, Ryan finally said, 'I've got it! No offense, but when you move on to something bigger and better, I'd like to be in your job.'"

"What did you say?"

"I told him that I was glad to hear that and that aggressive growth was what J.D. wanted from both of us. I said I thought it was still a couple of years away, but that I would be happy to help him on that path. This gave me a natural segue to the third question: 'How do you need to change to achieve your goals in the future state?'"

"And his reply?"

"Ryan thought for a moment and then said, 'I know I need to be more focused and not allow emotions to affect my decisions, and I'm open to any input or ideas that you could give on that front.' He said he had hesitated to ask me for advice like this in the past out of fear that I would just tell him to worry about his quota and keep his focus on managing his accounts. I agreed that that probably would have been my response and that communication between the two of us needed to improve—and I acknowledged that that improvement needed to start with me. I told him that I would do my best to help in any way that I could, and that's where we concluded the meeting. But I have to tell you, Owen, that really hurt to hear."

"I'll bet."

"I had no idea that I had been sending that kind of disempowering message to one of the members of my team, but obviously I had. Hearing Ryan say that was a real gut-check moment for me. It was a reinforcement of what you've been telling me about creating trust within the team and about my most important job being to develop my people. It is crystal clear to me now that I had an unhealthy obsession with numbers and what they said about me, and that obsession caused me to neglect my own people. It's clear that I've got to work on myself through this process as well."

Owen said, "That's a great insight, Tom, and I'm already

seeing lots of progress. We'll get there. You've got your follow-up plans in place with all your people, correct?"

"Yep—the times and deliverables are all documented in my binder and ready for review."

"OK, great. Let me suggest that next week you and I get together at the Bradgate corporate offices and we bring J.D. up to date on what we've been doing so far."

"Great. I'll see you then. Do I need to bring anything?"

"How about your own job description?" Owen said. "You may want to give Ryan a copy. While you're at it, maybe have him do an analysis comparing his current level of experience and the job requirements."

Tom nodded and said, "Sounds like a plan."

Big Ideas

- It is part of your job to develop your people and to identify career goals that motivate and inspire them.
- If you don't already have them, create written job descriptions for yourself and all the team members who report to you.

Be Intentional about a Succession Plan

Some managers would be threatened by an employee who expresses interest in their position. The intentional manager recognizes that it is their role to develop people for advancement, assuming that is the person's career goal.

Note that the manager's opportunity for advancement is often contingent on the leadership's belief that there is a strong candidate available to replace the manager. The concept of succession planning is often ignored or neglected by managers because of the complexity of the subject and the many variables involved: changes in organizational structure, unexpected departures and adjustments, and shifting career goals being just a few. Suppose, for instance, that an employee who was on the management development track unexpectedly decides that they are no longer willing to relocate.

Ironically, the complexity of the issue and the many variables involved only serve to underscore why succession planning is so important. A manager who is intentional about developing and promoting their people knows how to position the discussion about advancement so that it is in line with the individual's career goals but does not put the company in an awkward situation. Of course, this takes practice and the willingness to learn over time, but it is nevertheless a critical element of your responsibility to develop your people so that they will stick around and contribute to their fullest potential. An intentional sales manager understands that the company's employees are its most important resource.

CHAPTER 14

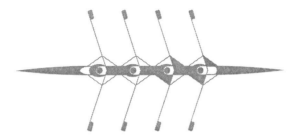

Turning the Corner

As Tom entered the Bradgate corporate building, he could sense a certain something in the air. It was hard to say exactly what it felt like. Possibility? Focus? Positive intent? Whatever it was, it felt stronger than it had felt the day before, which was when he'd first noticed it. He smiled and made his way to the break room.

The odd, intangible energy he was picking up on could have come from the members of his team, or it could have been his own feeling of optimism based on the results of the last week, which had been more encouraging than anything he'd seen in months. It could have been a combination of the two. The updates the team had been sharing with him informally, on their own initiative, had all been positive, and the feeling of trust in the department was beginning to build. Tom had a sense the salespeople were plugging into the work he'd been doing with Owen, and the level of optimism in the department was beginning to build. Tom sat back and enjoyed a stress-free morning coffee to start his day.

Tom saw Owen walking down the hall and waved to him.

"Good morning Owen—good to see you!" said Tom.

"Great to see you, too, Tom." Owen took the last sip of his coffee and caught up with Tom, smiling as they shook hands. "Not too early, I hope."

"Not at all. So glad you could come down today. Hey, before you and I get started, J.D. said he would like to meet with us very briefly. Are you OK with that?"

"Absolutely," said Owen. "Let's go." They made their way up to the corner office. Tom knocked on J.D.'s open door.

As J.D. looked up from his computer, Tom said, "Is this still a good time? Owen is here."

"Sure," J.D. said, as he came from behind the desk to shake Owen's hand. He gestured for them to sit at the conference table, and took a seat at its head. "I'm hearing good things," J.D. said. "I could sense last week that Tom was headed in the right direction, and the discussions I've been having with him and with the members of his team all seem to be positive. You guys must have been busy!"

"We have," Tom said.

"Yes," Owen said. "As you know, it's a process, and it's not something that you finish off in a month or two. But I do have to say that I'm very happy with Tom's buy-in and engagement and with the results we've been seeing from the team."

"Me, too," J.D. said. "Having said that, though, I want to own up to something important. I know that I'm part of the equation here—just like my CEO was part of the equation back when you worked with me, Owen."

Hmm, Tom thought. *I knew J.D. used to run the sales department, but I had no idea that he had worked with Owen. It's probably just as well that I didn't know—that might have spooked me just a bit. Anyway—J.D. is clearly doing well professionally. Maybe working with Owen had something to do with that.*

Owen said, "Your instincts are right on target, J.D. The process is taking hold, and we're about to start looking in-depth at Tom's personal development. It's fortuitous that you asked to talk to me this morning because I was going to suggest that you take part in this next discussion. I think it would be helpful if Tom and I heard more about your expectations of his role, both in the current and future state. Once we have clarity about that we will be in a better position to set his personal key performance indicators. Can you tell us a little bit more about what it is exactly you expect?"

"Sure, I'd be happy to discuss KPIs," J.D. said, as he leaned back in his chair, "but before we get into that, can I ask you guys a question?"

"Sure," Owen said. Tom nodded.

"I looked at the most recent sales results and I see only a modest improvement. Should I be concerned about that?"

Owen gave Tom a look that said, "I'll handle this," and then looked back at J.D. "Remember," Owen said, "this process is all about looking at behaviors as the leading indicators. The results will come."

"And how are those looking?" J.D. asked.

Tom said, "We're seeing steady increases on the new appointments and on the lead conversions. I'm very, very happy with the trends on those numbers."

"OK, good," J.D. said. "You know, Owen, I do remember that from back when you were coaching me. Sometimes I forget my own history, though, because I'm looking at the company revenue results on a monthly basis through a historical lens. I guess that would be a lagging indicator, though, wouldn't it?"

"That's correct," Owen said.

"Alright," J.D. said, "I'll trust you guys to handle the details."

"Great," Owen said. "Now let's talk about your expectations of Tom."

"Yes. So as far as that goes, I see Tom's primary role as developing his people so that the company gets full benefit of their talents and performance. That's number one. Secondly, another expectation is for him to continuously learn and develop as a professional and as a leader. Finally, I want him to know his numbers and know what is affecting them—with the ability to adjust where necessary in order to reach the plan."

Tom nodded in agreement.

"Now, hopefully," J.D. continued, "none of these expectations come as a surprise."

"Nope," Tom answered. "Not one of them. You've been clear about your expectations since day one, J.D., and I'm very grateful for that. I just didn't have the full skill set I needed, and I didn't know where to turn for the resources."

J.D. nodded and said, "We've all been there, Tom. In my experience, it's the managers who are willing to admit that they need help and then reach out and get that help who tend to thrive and succeed over time. I've seen way, way too many people refuse to seek out help because they were afraid of appearing vulnerable. That turned out to be their downfall."

"I can attest to that one," Owen said. "I've seen it play out many times. J.D., unless you have anything else for us, we'll get to work on Tom's goals and let you get back to running the company."

Back in Tom's office, Owen opened his laptop.

"Ready to get to work?" Owen asked.

"You bet," said Tom.

Owen created three columns and typed three words across the top of the pages. They would use the words as categories to capture J.D.'s expectations.

PEOPLE	PROFESSIONAL	PLAN

Owen turned to Tom and said, "Here is where we can brainstorm about behaviors for each category. What I'm hoping we can do is come up with a whole lot of great ideas and then prioritize the top three or four in each of these categories and use them to build your daily accountability plan. Shall we get started?"

"Let's do it," Tom answered.

After nearly two hours of kicking around ideas, they had distilled their initial list of several dozen possibilities down to a manageable summary of a few key behaviors in each of the three categories. Their summary looked like this.

People

1. Develop an individual training needs analysis for each salesperson and identify a resource or action for each to accomplish quarterly.
2. Identify one technique for each salesperson to master—not just understand—each month.

3. Debrief two sales calls per week with each salesperson.

Professional

1. Listen to at least one podcast per week on leadership or management.
2. Read two business books per month.
3. Attend one professional development seminar per quarter.

Plan

1. Establish and review key sales production numbers daily.
2. Track the activity of all the salespeople weekly.
3. Measure the effectiveness of sales activities weekly (i.e., compare each salesperson's behaviors to the trends needed to achieve personal goals).

Owen said, "That's a good start. We can refine the activities as you start to develop some history."

Tom nodded. "I've never really scheduled time to do any of this in the past. The new routine will certainly keep me busy."

"That's true," acknowledged Owen, "but I think you'll be surprised at how many hours you win back in the work day once you're focused on good activities and you learn to avoid the roles of Chief Problem Solver and Panic Manager-in-Chief."

Tom smiled. "I suspect you're right," he said.

Owen saved the document and closed the laptop. "Now, before we go any further, Tom," he said, "I've got to ask you some questions."

"Really?" Tom suddenly felt a little twist in his stomach. What was this all about?

Owen paused for a moment, and then smiled. "Tom, you know this checklist doesn't mean anything until I ask you the following: Why do you work the way you do? What do you want to achieve? And how do you need to change to achieve your goals in the future state?"

A look of relief came over Tom's face. "I've actually been giving these questions a good deal of thought."

"I'm not surprised. I'll bet you knew this moment was coming."

"Let's just say I had a feeling it might. The truth is, I came up with the answer to that first question fairly easily. I work the way I do because that is all I know. Period. I was raised in a blue-collar household where hard work was a given. As I began my career and moved from position to position, all my managers used basically the same approach, setting the goal based on a sales number and measuring the team's performance against the sales results. I realize now that these numbers are outcomes of specific behaviors that can be tracked. All the hard work I did as a manager was focused on fixing the same types of problems each week. I guess at some psychological level I was satisfying my 'work hard' script by fixing problems because I didn't know what else to do."

"What do you want to achieve now?" Owen asked.

"I've thought about that, too," Tom said. "What I most want to achieve..." Tom paused and looked to the ceiling for some reason, realizing for the first time that the pattern of the tiles was not aligned. He took a deep breath, and then, looking back at Owen, said, "What I want most is to be recognized as a leader here at Bradgate and within our industry."

Owen said, "That is a noble aspiration, but I have to ask—why? Why is that important to you?"

Tom seemed ready for the question. "A number of reasons," he said. "I owe it to the company and my colleagues to be the best I can be as part of a team. If I'm not utilizing my talents and growing, I'm doing them a disservice. Next, if I'm asking my people to be their best, then I've got to lead by example. Have you ever heard that saying—I think it's from Ralph Waldo Emerson? 'The speed of the leader determines the rate of the pack.'"

"Good point," Owen observed.

"Finally, I want to do it for myself as a means of reinvigorating my career. In the past when I had ambitious and meaningful goals, I've aligned them. I've achieved them and enjoyed the journey. Somehow when I got here to Bradgate, I became fixated on the tasks and the numbers without linking them to goal outcomes."

"Trust me. You're not the first to have that experience," Owen said.

"Good to know. Now I bet we have to assign behaviors to the goal, so that I'm accountable and the progress can be tracked. Am I right?"

"That's right," said Owen. "I think you're beginning to own the process, so why don't you assign the behaviors and their frequency to make up your intentional manager plan and email it to me by this Friday? That way, we can discuss them during our next session."

"Sounds good," said, Tom. "I've got some ideas, but I would definitely want your input on any additional things I could do to be a top-performing leader."

Big Ideas

- Create a list of quantifiable (countable) behaviors that support the goal of being a resource for the team.
- Create a list of quantifiable behaviors that support your goal of developing yourself professionally.
- Create a list of quantifiable behaviors that support your goal of executing the quarterly (and annual) sales plan.

Be Intentional about Managing Your Own Growth

It's vitally important to track the right metrics. Often, leaders of organizations focus their attention on outcomes or results. For instance: "What deals just closed? What deals are just about to close?" While these are fair questions, they're not the only metrics you want to track when it comes to the sales team. These are lagging indicators—they only give us a rearview mirror look at what has already happened. Notice that lots of things have to take place in order for a deal to reach the point where it's going to close. For instance, there are all those initial conversations with prospects with whom the salesperson hasn't yet interacted. What if you measured those, too? How many happen each working day? How many need to happen each working day?

When you're dealing with salespeople, you want to measure the leading indicators—the behaviors that produce future income—not just the lagging indicators. Precisely the same principle holds true for sales managers. You can't just look at the deals that are closing. You need to look closely at the best metrics, or key performance indicators (KPIs), for that manager.

These are going to be the KPIs that correlate to early activities that are likely to support team success. The best measures of a sales leader's effectiveness are the critical, measurable activities entirely under the person's control that create and sustain a positive team culture—and lead to successful outcomes for the salespeople. For instance:

- Number of structured one-on-one coaching sessions conducted.
- Number of ride-alongs.
- Number of post-sale debriefings completed.

Many sales managers, it should be emphasized, evolve from a sales role. As a salesperson, it is easy to measure your impact because of metrics related to sales volume, dollar amounts, averages, ratios, and new accounts.

When managers accept their new responsibility as a sales leader, they are told to do things like set the strategy, define the culture, and develop their people. These are all are critical to the role of manager, but they are also activities that have a long-term perspective. What will you be doing each day? You can easily edge your way back into being a senior salesperson unless you are intentional about staying in the manager role. Indeed, that is the most common pattern.

The main reason for this problem seems to come down to a manager's need to feel like a contributor to the end goal, as they were when they were an individual contributor. There could also be a comfort zone issue, which would suggest that the manager is feeling lost in their role and reverting back to their sales capacity because this allows them to stay busy in familiar ways. Unfortunately, these have an adverse effect on the sales department. Salespeople can become overly dependent on the manager to set up or close sales for them or to take responsibility for developing major opportunities.

Another common problem is the manager may neglect the roles of coaching, training, and holding people accountable, focusing solely on the mentoring role and expecting behavioral change to occur simply because the salesperson has spent time in their presence.

Growth as a manager can be an elusive quest until the manager begins to realize just how much they don't know. This challenge is sometimes referred to as the circle of ignorance—the larger the circle gets, the more aware you are of how much you don't know.

Turning the Corner

A manager who operates in the figurative tight circle will think that they know all or nearly all there is to know about being a manager or leader. It is not until they expand their understanding that they become aware of how much more they still have to learn. The truly intentional manager quickly realizes that learning and growth are interchangeable and that they must never stop either one. Other managers, by contrast, learn only enough to sustain themselves in their first management assignment and then, sadly, come to believe that they have arrived and they have no need to learn further or look for a coach who can help them learn to show vulnerability. Don't be one of them!

CHAPTER 15

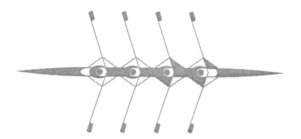

The Team Meeting, Transformed

It had been a couple of months since Tom had first sat down one-on-one with each of his salespeople. The format of the team sales meetings had changed dramatically since then. No longer was the focus on the department's production numbers and each salesperson's updates on each of the accounts in their pipeline. (Those discussions were held for the private meetings, which had a clear coaching focus.) The team sales meetings now followed an agenda based on input of the sales team. The salespeople had told Tom that they wanted to be updated about company issues and also that they wanted to master, with

Tom's help, the top ten behaviors of successful sales professionals. With Tom's facilitation, they agreed to work as a group on these top ten behaviors, all of which support the performance of top performing salespeople.

1. Lead generation
2. Building relationships
3. Qualifying opportunities
4. Making presentations
5. Serving customers
6. Account management
7. Territory development
8. Building a plan for success
9. Continuous learning
10. Execution of a proven selling system

Each team sales meeting was facilitated by a team member—not by Tom. Today's meeting was facilitated by Ryan. It was his turn to research and present techniques and concepts relating to item number three, qualifying.

In doing his own research and personal development work, he had come across a principle he had learned at a recent training program. He started the meeting by reading it aloud for the group: "'Your success and ultimately your commission is determined more by the information you gather, rather than the information you dispense.'" Ryan went on to explain that he had realized during a one-on-one meeting with Tom that this rule had particular application to his own selling routine.

"I discovered," Ryan said, "that my knowledge of the company's product and service line and my desire to help were combining to form a toxic formula for talking and not listening. I was putting prospects off and answering questions they hadn't asked. In some cases, I was sharing so much information that I was teaching people how to work with my competitors. During our coaching discussion, Tom helped me realize the importance of asking rather than telling. I started learning from him about the importance of qualifying. The result has been a significantly shortened sales cycle and a much healthier pipeline. So the big tip I want to share with you today is to make sure we understand the prospect's reasons and ability to buy from us—before we start telling them how we're going to provide them with a solution."

Tom thanked Ryan for his facilitation. Then he asked if any of the salespeople had questions for Ryan.

Camila raised her hand, "Yes, I have a question."

Ryan said, "OK—what have you got?"

Camila responded with something she apparently had been thinking about for quite a while. "How are we supposed to qualify when the prospect just asked for our proposal and it's a big opportunity?"

Tom, of course, said nothing. This was Ryan's meeting.

Ryan paused, looked at Camila and, instead of answering the question, asked her a question. (This technique is known as "reversing.") "Camila," he said, "I'm curious. Do you ever feel like the prospect is in control when you are both involved in the sales process?"

"Yes," she said. "After all, they make the decisions and they have the right to decide. Not to mention they have the money that I'm trying to get!"

As she smiled and others politely chuckled at her comment, Ryan said, "Do you recall item number one from our top ten list?"

Camila said, "Not offhand, but I've got my sheet here in my notebook. Yes, here it is. Item number one is lead generation."

Ryan said, "Good. Now, while you have the sheet out, can you read number eight for us?"

"Number eight: building a plan for success," she said, with an inflection that made it sound as much like a question as it did a statement.

Ryan went on, "I don't know if the rest of you noticed, but there is an interrelationship between a number of the items on our list. I discovered it almost by accident. I found myself relying on social media as a means of developing new prospects. While I thought that was fairly effective, it occurred to me that I had ignored other lead generation activities Tom and I had identified as being important.

"It wasn't long before I noticed that my new prospect meetings were becoming fewer and fewer. As that happened, I began to feel more desperate to close deals. I began to skip qualifying questions—out of a fear that the truth might disqualify the prospect. Eventually I found my prospect pipeline full of companies that I had sent proposals to, but that I hadn't heard back from. I spent a great deal of time and energy trying to re-engage with prospects—because I had invested so much time and effort in them already.

"As I was stalking a prospect one afternoon, I noticed the plan for success that Tom and I had developed together. It was sitting on my desk, in my in-basket. I picked it up and began to read it—and the metaphorical light bulb in my head went on. I realized I was not doing the behaviors at a level that allowed me to get enough prospects—and the few 'prospects' I had were not qualified to become my customer. Does that make sense? I know it was a long answer, Camila, but I want you to know I can relate to what you'd just asked."

Camila said, "Yes. I see what you mean. Thank you so much for that. It makes total sense." She abruptly turned to Tom and said, "Can I schedule one of those planning meetings with you soon?"

Tom said, "You sure can. I would've suggested it earlier, but you didn't seem ready."

Camila said, "Oh, I'm ready." And she smiled.

As Ryan took his seat at the large conference table, Keiko said, "You know, Ryan, I noticed the connection between a number of the items on our list as well. For example, item number two, building relationships, definitely plays into qualifying. It also applies to making presentations. I find that the more I focus on the issues and challenges of the prospect and the more questions I ask about both the problem and the person, the more likely I am to nail number four, making presentations."

Probably because he did not want to feel left out and was hoping to contribute something to the meeting, Jason said, "You know, as I look at the list, I can also see a link between building relationships and item number five, servicing customers. Based on the relationships that I have built with recent prospects who became clients, I was able to direct operations and our support team on the best ways to service new accounts."

Tom sat back and smiled as the team shared ideas and best practices among themselves. He made a mental note to tell Owen that he owed him a great deal of gratitude as his team was beginning to function just as he had promised it would.

As the conversation slowed, Tom looked at his phone, checked the time, and then said, "OK, folks, great job. We'll reconvene the same time next week. Jason, you've got next week's meeting—the focus is on item number four, making presentations. In the meantime, let's get out there and work on item number one, lead generation."

They all stood up and charged the door like a football team after a halftime pep talk. As Stace walked past Tom, Tom said, "Stace, can you stay back? I'd like to get caught up on some things." As the others filed out, Tom leaned over and pushed the door closed. He looked at Stace and motioned for her to be seated.

Tom could see the look of concern in Stace's eyes so he quickly shared his intention for this one-on-one meeting. "Stace, I've been observing you for the last few months. You've made some progress on the things we talked about. Your prospect meetings are increasing. I'd like to see your closing ratio go up, but that will come in time if you're committed to this as your career—which leads me to my bigger question. Stace, I need you to level with me. Are you happy in this sales role?"

Stace stopped looking at Tom in the eye and looked down at the floor. She picked a piece of imaginary lint off her slacks and, after a long while, said, "No, Tom, if I'm being honest with you, I'd have to say I'm really not as happy as I could be in this role. I thought I would get used to it. I thought the money would make it all worthwhile. I am glad you brought this up because I've been thinking we might need to talk about it. I just don't think I'm cut out for sales. I find myself looking at other departments wishing that I could work in a role that doesn't have the same level of pressure and unpredictability, a role where I know what to do every day. Tom, I really love working here and

I'll stay in sales if that is what I have to do to keep working at Bradgate. But I really do think about working in other departments sometimes. That's my answer."

"I recognize that, Stace, and I appreciate you being honest with me."

"I guess I feel like I can trust you, Tom, and I wanted to give you a straight answer. If I have to leave, I will. But I would certainly like to keep working at Bradgate."

Tom said reassuringly, "Stace, you are recognized as a good employee here, and I know for a fact you have skills that we need. We just need to put you in a different role. Please understand. This was my issue, not yours, because I am the one who picked the wrong role for you in the first place. For now, please do keep working just like you have been, and let's keep this discussion between us. I will talk with HR to figure out the right place for you here at Bradgate, some place that's a better fit."

Stace said, "You've got it. Thanks for caring enough to ask about this."

Big Ideas

- Train, reinforce, and coach the top ten behaviors of successful salespeople. (They are covered in this chapter.)
- A great principle to share with salespeople is: "Your success and ultimately your commission is determined more by the information you gather, rather than the information you dispense."
- Some people don't belong on your sales team. That's life.

Be Intentional about Your Coaching Process

A nationally recognized trainer and sales coach, Bill Bartlett, developed the list of ten behaviors shared in this chapter. In his marvelous book *The Sales Coach's Playbook*, Bill does a great job of explaining why an understanding of these ten items are important to effective sales management and how to adapt and integrate them as priorities into just about any sales team in just about any business.

Bartlett's list can and should act as a guide for the tactical activities that must be mastered in support of an effective sales manager's strategic efforts on behalf of the team. In my experience, the absence of a list like this (tailored, of course, to your company and industry) will foster an unhealthy cycle in which the manager, knowingly or otherwise, creates both busy work and chaos—and, as a result, has something to "fix."

Intentional sales coaching requires a clear understanding of the behaviors required for success, as well as a strong self-awareness and a feeling of comfort in using good questions to help others see their blind spots, skill gaps, and less-than-supportive beliefs. None of this comes naturally. It must be studied and practiced over time, often with the guidance and support of a coach of your own.

CHAPTER 16

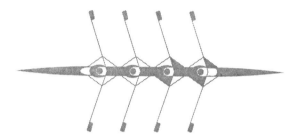

The Self-Correcting Team

Owen hadn't been to Tom's office in over a month. They had agreed that Tom's weekly updates about his progress in managing with intention and focusing on the sales team's goal accomplishments could be covered via email. Today's meeting, then, fell into the category they now called the "monthly face-to-face."

Tom waved Owen in as he stood in the doorway and motioned for him to be seated. He was just finishing a one-on-one call with Keiko, who was sharing the details of her latest win.

"Keiko, do you mind if I put you on speaker?"

Tom reached over and pushed the "group listen" feature on his phone so that Owen could hear both sides of the call. As her voice came through the speaker, Owen could hear her saying everything was "finally clicking."

"It was just like we've been practicing," Keiko continued, "because my pipeline is so full. I am sure they had the sense that I wanted their business, but I didn't need their business. When they brought up objections, I asked them to figure out how to overcome them. We must have spent 40 minutes with them coming up with all the possible challenges associated with switching to Bradgate, and then I let them convince themselves it was worth dealing with the challenges to get the solutions that we would offer. I had to do very little talking—exactly what you and Owen have been saying would happen. Periodically, I would just ask a simple question about all the problems they were dealing with, and then it was another 10 minutes about how serious they were about fixing the problems and how much they needed my help."

"That's great," said Tom, who noticed that Owen was smiling.

"It was just like one of our role-play scenarios," she continued. "I said, 'Let me summarize what I think I heard.' They said, 'Please. We've been doing all the talking.' I think they were looking for me to start telling them about our features and benefits to fix their problems. In reality, I just fed back to them

The Self-Correcting Team

what they had just said, making sure to include the most accurate dollar impact I could and leaving the problems unsolved. And then, as you have taught me, Tom, I looked them in the eye and asked them your two questions. 'Are you committed to fixing these problems?' They said yes. 'And, do you want my help?' They said yes to that, too."

Keiko's voice was jubilant. It sounded as though she had just won the lottery. Owen gave Tom a thumbs-up.

"Then," she continued, "they asked, 'How soon can you start?' I saw the president lean forward to sign our agreement. It was my first one-call close on a six figure deal, but I can tell you it won't be my last. Thanks again, Tom, for getting me motivated again, and for giving us the tools and new techniques to be successful. Hey, I've got to run to another appointment. Do you need anything else?"

"No," Tom said, "Keep up the good work."

"You can count on it," she said. There was a little click, and the speaker went quiet.

Owen said, "Very impressive. Tom. She seems to really be taking to the coaching that you've been providing, and she's clearly seeing the results. I've got to ask. She referred to 'your' two questions. Where did those come from?"

"Well, Keiko was concerned that her prospects were taking too long to make decisions. She figured out that to make her stretch goals, she had to do something differently. So after I had her share some specific examples, I suggested she ask those two questions consecutively. 'Are you committed to fixing these problems?' Followed by: 'Do you want my help?' Since she has been asking those, Keiko has seen her sales cycle reduce dramatically, and her forecasting has also improved significantly. They serve as elixirs to the truth. You should recognize them, Owen. They are the exact questions you asked me as you were helping me discover my own need to change. They were so effective getting me to commit that I figured they would work in the qualifying stages of a sales call."

"They do indeed," said Owen.

The phone rang. Tom instinctively looked at his caller ID screen. He then looked at Owen and said, "This will only take about a minute. It's HR—they're probably calling about Stace."

Owen gestured to the phone for Tom to pick it up, then he opened his portfolio to read some notes.

"Hey, Beth, any news?" There was a pause, then Tom smiled as he listened to the answer. After a few seconds, he said, "That's great. Is there a timeframe?" Tom checked the email on his laptop and said, "OK, I see your message now. I'll get with Stace and let her know. Thanks for all your help, Beth."

As Tom hung up the phone, he started talking to Owen as if he had heard the whole conversation: "That's good for Stace and customer relations—she will do very well in that role."

Owen said, "Oh, that's right. You and Stace agreed that she

wasn't a fit in sales, and you committed to finding her another position here at Bradgate."

"That's right. It all came together beautifully. It's kind of amazing how good it feels to help people reach their potential."

"I agree," Owen said with a smile. "What else is on your agenda this morning?"

Tom looked at his calendar and said, "Well, I've got the last weekly one-on-one call of the day with Ryan in five minutes, and then I have my monthly development meeting with J.D. He's keeping with the process you taught him. You should be proud."

"I am," Owen replied. "You know, I have to say this: It's amazing how good it feels to help people reach their potential." He winked at Tom.

Tom winked back.

The phone rang. It was Ryan, calling in at the appointed time. Tom asked Owen, "Do you want to listen in?"

Owen said, "Absolutely."

Tom hit the speaker button and said, "Good morning, Ryan. I'm here with Owen. OK if he listens in?"

Ryan said, "Sure. Then I'll have a witness when you start yelling at me," and laughed. Tom and Owen laughed, too.

When their laughter had subsided, Ryan said, "Owen, on a serious note, I do want to thank you for helping us turn the department around. I know it was rough at the beginning, but as Tom got committed, we all began to buy in and now it's really great working here. I feel more confident in the future, and I'm excited about my growth in the territory and my present prospect pipeline. Thanks again for introducing me to the training. It has had a huge impact on my behaviors, techniques, and attitude."

"I'm glad it's helped," Owen said, "but don't let me interrupt you and Tom. Please get on with your call as if I'm not here."

At that, Tom said, "Alright, Ryan, why don't you give me your top three prospect recaps? I've reviewed the email you sent that tallied your behaviors and KPIs. It looks like you are on track with your new prospect call volume, way over on your weekly goal for social media contacts, and slightly behind on referral requests. Is there anything you'd like to discuss about the email?"

Ryan said, "Yes, there is. I'm concerned that the KPI related to the ratio of 'calls made' to 'appointments booked' is below our target."

"Why do you think that is?"

Ryan said, "I'm not sure. In the past, it would start to go down if I was working a new territory or my calls were primarily from a database." There was a little pause, and then Ryan said, "That's it! I can't believe I missed it."

"Missed what?"

"It's right there," Ryan said. "Staring me in the face. I'm not asking for referrals at the rate I had been, and as a result, my conversion of calls to appointments is being impacted. I can assure you, that will be fixed, starting today."

"OK," Tom said. "Unless there is something else, are you ready to review your top prospects?"

"Sounds good," said Ryan. "I'll start with the one I need the most help with. Remember the prospect from the beginning of the year who wanted me to work up that big proposal before I spoke to any of the key stakeholders?"

"Yes. Weren't they up on the North Side?"

"Yep. That's the one. Briscoe Inc. Anyway, they reached out to me and asked me to come to their office."

"What for?" asked Tom.

"That's what I asked. Apparently the supplier that did give them a proposal without talking to anybody is now causing operational issues, and that means Briscoe is losing customers. My original contact is afraid he will lose his job if he doesn't fix the problem immediately. My concern is that he may not realize the importance of me talking to all the senior stakeholders, but I know they may still resist getting together to discuss that. How should I address that?"

Tom said, "Good job on stepping back and thinking this through so that you don't get trapped. Again, I know it is tempting to just jump in because it's a big opportunity. But let me ask, how qualified would you say they are right now to be your prospect?"

"I know they have the indication of the gap between where they are and where they want to be and they understand the impact of not taking action," Ryan said, "but I don't have any read on the decision-making process, and I don't understand the executive team's level of commitment to fix the problem." There was a tiny pause, and then Ryan's excited voice rang through the speaker: "Wait! That's it!"

"What's it?"

"I can use the commitment discussion as a logical reason, in my main contact's eyes, to open the dialogue with the executive team. I know he doesn't want to be in the hot seat any more regarding the problems with the current vendor. He can legitimately say that a solution is possible if they are committed enough to meet with us."

"And what if they aren't committed enough to meet with us?"

Ryan said, "Well, then, we can't help them. As you know, I'm hitting my numbers and have a healthy pipeline. That means I would like their business, but I don't need their business. If they are not willing to meet with a supplier at the beginning of a partnership, then unfortunately they are likely to keep repeating the mistakes of their past."

Tom smiled and then looked over to Owen with a gleam of

pride and appreciation. It was as if all they'd worked on creating together had just taken tangible form.

Ryan said, "Hello? You guys there?"

Tom realized he hadn't yet acknowledged Ryan's statement. "Ryan," he said, "you are absolutely on point. You have a realistic attitude about this opportunity. I agree with the tactics you plan to use, and it's clear to me your behaviors are consistent. That's the formula for success: attitude, tactics, and behavior. So—what about the other two prospects?"

"They are both in the early stages: ABC Media and Gramble Brands. Once I get them qualified, I may need you to make a joint call with me to illustrate our interest. They're both major opportunities. However, early indications are that they will follow our process so we probably won't be caught up in the same kind of wrestling match and power struggle as we did with Briscoe."

"OK. Keep me posted. Great job today, Ryan. Call me if you need me."

"I will. Thanks, Tom. Good talking to you, Owen." With that, the line went quiet. Tom picked up the receiver and dropped it back on the cradle to disconnect the line.

Tom and Owen sat silently for a while. Eventually Tom said, "You know, that really felt good. Eight months ago, I would have felt the need to tell Ryan 'I told you so' about the Briscoe problem or take credit when he figured out the strategy. I probably would have needed to add to his idea so that he noticed that I had the last word. But now with your help and coaching, I see my own role performance elevated when my people do well and when they care enough to think strategically and come up with their own ideas. I no longer feel the need to prove myself at the expense of my salespeople's self respect and confidence."

"Tom," Owen said, "you have definitely come a long way from that first day we met at the counter at the Crossroads Diner. For that, you do deserve credit, even though I know that is not what you are looking for. Over the past few months, you have been able to admit to a problem, measure the impact, and acknowledge the potential consequences. You have been willing to be humble enough to accept help, and you have changed the culture of your team by changing your own perspective on your role. Because of that, you built enough trust with your salespeople for them to be willing to accept your coaching and become more accountable. As a result, you have put yourself in a position to encourage the team to set their own goals, take ownership of their own growth, and follow development plans that they have helped to create. You've built a self-correcting team. Tom, you are now respected among your peers as a leader, and you are beginning to be recognized in your industry as an expert in developing a professional sales team. So can I make a suggestion?"

The Self-Correcting Team

Tom said, "By all means."

"Would you let me take you out to lunch so we can celebrate?"

"Sure," Tom said. "That sounds great. How about the Crossroads Diner?"

And that's exactly where they went.

> **Big Ideas**
>
> - Give credit wherever you can to individual team members. Don't claim credit for yourself.
> - You cannot possibly solve every problem. You are only successful as a manager to the degree that you support your team members' capacity to identify and resolve their own problems.

Be Intentional about Practice

Sales managers have the unique challenge of understanding what their people are doing and saying on a sales call, without actually being on most (or any) of those calls. An operations manager can observe and check production logs. An accounting manager can check the results against standard accounting practices. Yet sales managers have to depend on the interpretation of a call through the filter of the salesperson—unless, of course, they are on a joint call. Even then, many sales managers have shared with me the confusion and disbelief they have experienced after making a joint call and hearing the salesperson, during the debrief, "remember" things that weren't said, questions that were never asked, and conclusions that were never implied.

To combat this problem and avoid the depressing feeling you have to find some way to be on every call (impossible, of course!), you may want to create the routine, during one-on-one sessions, of role-playing to address whatever areas of difficulty the salesperson is having. Initially, this may be uncomfortable for both of you. Be intentional. Do it anyway. After a series of sessions and a buildup of trust, you will find that

The Self-Correcting Team

salespeople will not only accept role-play sessions, but request them. Always remember, though, that it is the manager's job to take the lead and initiate role-plays in the early stages.

During a role-play session, you must be at the top of your game. That means you must be patient, encourage the salesperson, be empathetic, be tactful, and give feedback to the salesperson that they can understand, accept, and act on. Also, the role-play sessions must be private. Make the enhancement of the salesperson's self-confidence your priority, and the development will follow.

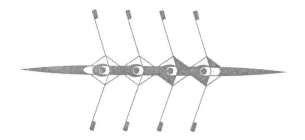

Epilogue

I hope you have enjoyed this book. Now you have a choice—the same choice everyone has whenever they acquire knowledge: What action will you take based on the ideas you have encountered here?

All too often, managers hear of a new technique or approach that can help their team or organization, and they think, *Wow—that is a great way to be more effective. I ought to give that a try.* And then what happens? Nothing changes.

Unfortunately, most people aren't very good at making sustainable, constructive change in their professional or personal lives without help. It's easy to read a book. The reality is, it's hard to make a big change all on your own.

Just as Tom needed a different perspective and a coach to help him think through things, build accountability, and develop new habits, you may need that as well. At Sandler Training, we help managers by meeting them where they are based on their challenges and their growth goals. We help them to define the attitude or mindset required to grow, along with the behaviors and techniques that support higher levels of performance.

The Sandler® Success Triangle provides the blueprint to a successful coaching relationship. Its three points are the attitude, behavior, and techniques capable of eliminating the role performance gaps you and your team face. Recognition of the interrelatedness of all three elements is the key to exponential growth.

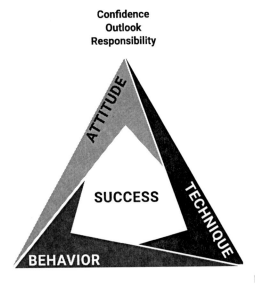

Our training program gives managers the tools they need to effect positive change by using the essential elements of the adult learning model. The steps of the adult learning model are:

- Knowledge acquisition
- Belief of fit
- Practice
- Real world application, culminating, over time, in mastery.

Where many people fall short is in the application or practice step. They try to implement what they've learned without a coach to guide them through the discomfort of creating a new habit or developing and refining a new skill. As a result, they revert back to the performance level they were at before they learned about the new way of doing things.

I can't tell you how many times I've seen this happen. It is very, very difficult to resist the psychological pull back to comfort zones, also known as habits. Everyone needs help with that.

After nearly two decades as a Sandler trainer and 15-plus years of sales and sales management in the corporate world, my experience is that those who are coachable and accountable are far more likely to succeed in sales management at a high level. With coaching comes the willingness, and the strength, to be vulnerable. With coaching comes the ability to be accountable to oneself in the pursuit of goals that really matter.

The learning model I have just shared with you, supported by a solid coaching relationship, is the success formula of top performers. For half a century now, Sandler Training has been helping professionals use that formula to reach greater heights of achievement by leveraging the Success Triangle, by clearly identifying company and individual goals, and by closing the gap between the current state and the future state. Seeing this powerful formula in action has been a tremendous honor for me. Let me give you just a couple of examples of the extraordinary results it has delivered.

Some years ago, I started working with a technology firm that had revenues of $3.8 million annually. The owner's leadership team were in agreement on this critical point: If they were going to be a significant player in their market, they needed consistent growth in terms of professional development. The leaders went first. They worked on improving communication and creating and sustaining an environment of trust. The employees noticed the changes and became much more encouraged about the future than they had been. Some of the employees were not able to embrace the changes that leadership had in mind and chose to leave the company within three years. Those who remained, however, saw the company culture change to one of unity rather than a "me first" approach based

Epilogue

on narrowly defined personal goals. The new company culture, the new team approach, and the Sandler Selling System® methodology enabled the company to increase its revenues to $6.4 million. Revenue has climbed steadily each year since, yielding an average growth rate of 27 percent.

Another example of the Sandler process in action came at a national brand whose leaders recognized that their own management style was a hindrance to growth—and was negatively affecting the company culture. Why had this happened? The company had grown by acquisition, and many managers remained loyal only to their past colleagues. This situation caused intense politicking, dissension, and eventually, paralyzing dysfunction among the brand's 3,000-plus employees. After six months of consultation, gap analysis, and transparent conversations, the leaders established a unified vision and positioned themselves to lead each of their divisions to achieve their true potential. This phase was followed by assessments of each and every one of those 3,000 employees for competencies and communication styles. The assessment data was then used to design group training, curriculum, and individual coaching plans.

The result has been a dramatic reduction of turnover among valued employees—down 46 percent—and an increase in average revenue per employee from $134,000 to $305,000.

Those are both remarkable success stories. There are hundreds more that are just as dramatic in the Sandler archives.

If you are concerned that your company or your team is not reaching its full potential and if you're willing to commit to persevere through the growing pains, you should know that Sandler Training is there for you. We have helped thousands of companies. We may be able to help your company, but we won't know unless we talk. Let's talk about your path forward as a sales leader. It's amazing how good it feels to help people reach their full potential!

Visit us at www.sandler.com.

Look for these other books on shop.sandler.com:

SALES SERIES
The Art and Skill of Sales Psychology
Asking Questions the Sandler Way
Bootstrap Selling the Sandler Way
Call Center Success the Sandler Way
Digital Prospecting
The Contrarian Salesperson
LinkedIn the Sandler Way
Prospect the Sandler Way
Retail Success in an Online World
Sandler Enterprise Selling
The Sandler Rules
The Unapologetic Saleswoman
Why People Buy
You Can't Teach a Kid to Ride a Bike at a Seminar

MANAGEMENT SERIES
Change the Sandler Way
Customer Service the Sandler Way
Lead When You Dance
Motivational Management the Sandler Way
Misery to Mastery
The Right Hire
The Road to Excellence
The Sales Coach's Playbook
The Sandler Rules for Sales Leaders
The Success Cadence
Transforming Leaders the Sandler Way
Winning from Failing

MOTIVATIONAL SERIES
Accountability the Sandler Way
From the Board Room to the Living Room
Sandler Success Principles
Succeed the Sandler Way

INDUSTRY SERIES
Making Channel Sales Work
Patient Care the Sandler Way
Selling in Manufacturing and Logistics
Selling Professional Services the Sandler Way
Selling to Homeowners the Sandler Way
Selling Technology the Sandler Way

Sandler Training

DEALING WITH
DIFFICULT PEOPLE | ONLINE COURSE

A step-by-step process to achieve positive outcomes.

You have undoubtedly experienced situations similar to the following:

- "What's wrong with you people? You never get it right!"
- "This is the last straw. I'm through doing business here."
- "Can't you break the rules for me this one time? I'm a good customer here!"

Sandler's online self-study course will help you:

 Self-assess your current automated response.

 Avoid the "he said, she said" scenario and manage expectations.

 Learn how judgment, triggers and egos can cloud the situation.

 Discover the difference between collaborative and combative negotiations.

Enroll in this course today!

Go to **sandler.com/peopleskills** and use promo code **BOOK-DWDP** to receive a special discounted offer!